Praise for "7 Times ⸝

– Moira Hutchison: M⸝

Thanks so much for allowing me to read your book. Although a bit hard to read at times due to the trauma and harshness, I found it to be an essential and transformative read. You really showed a tenacious commitment to bringing your message to the world and I think you will inspire much healing and help people to connect to their own sense of divinity.

– Anil Agrawal: Business Coach –

Holly's stories demonstrate one thing–human spirit knows no bounds. In each of the seven stories, Holly vividly narrates the scene in graphical detail. You virtually visualize each scene as if you are watching a movie. You witness her struggle and how she survived and lived on. She just never gave up. After each horrendous experience, she moved on, much stronger each time. Holly even came close to dying, but spirits showed up to remind her that she must live and serve her real purpose in life. Holly's stories are simply captivating. I would read each story sitting on the edge of my seat, wonder about what's to become of Holly, and jump with joy when the story concluded and Holly made a heroic exit alive and unfazed. Holly's tales are a metaphor for the tough realities of life. She has amply demonstrated how one should step up to the plate, muster courage and never give up in difficult times.

– Keith Thomsen –

Holly's life story shows that a person is not defined by those bad things that happen to them but how that person responds to those events. Holly repeatedly comes back from many an incident that a lesser person would have given up on life as a result, and shows that by "keeping moving forward" and learning from what has happened, one can find their way to their life's purpose as a result.

7 Times Saved

How One Woman's Spiritual Connections to the Other Side Saved Her Life.

Cover Design: Timothy Hann

This publication is designed to provide an accurate account of one individual's experiences. It is sold with the understanding that the author is not engaged in rendering counselling, legal, or other professional services. If legal advice or other expert assistance is required, the services of a professional should be sought.

7

Times Saved

How One Woman's Spiritual Connections to the Other Side Saved Her Life

HOLLY A. KLINE

True Stories of One Woman's Life-Saving
Encounters with the Spirit World and
Her Will to Survive

To My Readers

To everyone who has turned tragedies into testimonials, disappointments into achievements, agony into motivation, I salute you!

I pray that you will find comfort in my shared experiences and that this book expands your awareness of the spiritual realm while you continue to *"Keep Moving Forward"* with your Spiritual Guides protecting and guiding you.

Disclaimer

The story you are about to read is my true-life story. Names have been changed to protect the confidentiality of others. When I refer to God, I am referencing the highest level of Spiritual Being with powers greater than those of ordinary humans.

This book is dedicated to
my children and grandchildren,
especially my grandson, Gordon.

I love you all!

CONTENTS

INTRODUCTION

Why I Wrote This Book

Welcome to the true story of my life and the seven times I almost died, but was saved by spiritual powers that gave me the strength to keep moving forward.

I realized my story needed to be told when I'd finally accepted what I was meant to do with my life—to motivate others to believe in the powers of the goodness of the spiritual world and to inspire them to never settle: don't settle for the life status you are "born into" and don't settle for society's standards for what you need to do to be successful. In chasing my better life, I wandered off the path that was meant for me many times, and each time I was nudged back to my true calling. These nudges took the forms of voices, visions, dreams, and visitations. What I realize now, looking back, is that I never listened to the gentle nudges, and it took these seven life-threatening instances that actually made me make a serious change in my life. Some of us are just more hard-headed than others!

In this autobiographical book, I share my stories of the seven life-threatening instances, which I survived and, moreover, I bounced back to life. These experiences—connections to the spiritual realm—guided me to who I am today, the work I do, and this book. I have crossed over to the other side and met angels and spiritual guides who helped me find my life purpose and the will to live, and in this book I share that with you.

Please note: This book is not for those who are triggered by violence, particularly child abuse.

Who Should Read This Book

This book, *7 Times Saved: How One Woman's Spiritual Connections to the Other Side Saved Her Life*, is an account of my own true experiences. My stories are a personal recounting of the spiritual interventions bestowed on me, and the resources and messages delivered to me that saved my life multiple times through which my life's purpose became revealed. This book was written for those who are intrigued about spiritual encounters and near-death experiences, and who want to find the courage to look beyond convention and overcome whatever is holding you back from living your true purpose.

Spiritual encounters and near-death experiences have become increasingly more absorbed into today's culture and more prevalent among today's spiritual leaders. Their followers are seeking guidance and support through various culturally acceptable practices including prayer, meditation, and professional support. Individuals are also seeking remedial intervention through new age treatments and psychic readings to guide them through daily lives and traumatic events.

Media, scholars, researchers, publishers, film producers, and even scientists are increasingly supporting such stories of spiritual and near-death experiences. Researchers have done empirical studies only to find that many individuals who have had a near-death experience return with a deeper connection to a higher power and a heightened respect for life. In daily living, the practice of meditation also helps us seek a deep inner connection to our core and our spiritual, higher self.

Themes

You will find several themes that show up multiple times in this book. They include the following:

Mediumship

Some mediums develop their skills through peaceful meditation and communion with the other side. For myself, I've been hearing voices and been given spiritual guidance my whole life, but it wasn't until my last life-threatening, traumatic event—one that left me temporarily paralyzed—that brought me to my spiritual path and taught me to accept myself as a medium to help others.

Messages from the Other Side

Each time I had one of these experiences, I came back to the physical world with more insight, thanks to messages from the other side. In some cases they not only helped me, but also my loved ones.

Spirit Guides

Throughout my life many spirits, entities, and guides have visited me. I heard these voices at a young age and had been captivated by just how many spirits really dealt with us on a daily basis. The Archangel Gabriel, who appears in the first chapter, gently announced in a loving voice who he was and his mission for me. Since then, I have had multiple guides, one being my mother once she passed and one being a kindred soul from my past life who saved me during some of my life-threatening situations.

God Has Bigger Plans

From when I was young, and had to learn that God wanted me to live for a purpose, to when I was older and lost what I thought was my dream job within the Canadian Federal Government, this book illustrates that it doesn't matter what our intentions are, God has bigger plans for us.

Divine Intervention

I experienced times when a potentially fatal incident is stopped by an unknown source, putting me in a physical position of safety so I would avoid any (or further) injury.

Out-of-Body Experiences

I had several experiences when my spirit disengaged from my broken body, but my spirit did not attempt to cross over. Instead, it stayed near the physical realm to speak with other spirits or to watch over the situation at hand.

Near-Death Experiences

These experiences are the times when I flat-lined and technically "died." My spirit fully crossed over or almost crossed over to the other side, but then came back to enter my physical body.

The Seven Life-Threatening Instances

Each of the situations I describe in this book had a significant impact on my life, some in more ways than one. I understand that many passages might not be easy to read, but it is in these stories that deeper meaning can be found. I hope they will be able to serve as a reflection for you to find meaning in your own hard times.

#1 SEEING GABRIEL

In my first life-threatening instance, I learned that we are sent here for a reason, and despite horrible conditions, we live life based on God's timeline, not our own. In this experience, I also learned the importance of forgiveness, and letting go of negative emotions such as anger and hatred. This situation set the groundwork for me to understand that I was responsible for saving myself, and for developing a spiritually positive attitude toward others, no matter what they might do to me. During regular beatings from my mother, I began to recite the prayer: "Dear God, forgive her as she does not know what she is doing." This allowed the source of negativity to shrink within me and, eventually, become eliminated. This early experience set the foundation for my spirituality. I learned that people would come in and out of my life, but ultimately, it was totally up to me to decide which path I was going to travel and choose my spiritual destiny; my legacy for both myself and my descendants. I learned that even though I tried to be a good girl for my mother, in the end it didn't matter. You can't get another person to love you no matter who or what they are to you. Therefore, it is more important to love oneself and to rise above what is left behind. The past can't be changed, and the future is up to you. I had to make friends with the past, as it had become a part of me.

#2 DOWN RANGE

This story is about my narrow escape from death from a point blank shooting at the firing range in a military training base. As the first bullet from the rifle of the soldier next to me flew barely a foot away from my head, someone or something pushed me down to protect me from being shot at. Even as I clutched the ground face down, I came awfully close to being shot to death— the remaining bullets from his rifle passed within inches of my body. As I lay there and prayed for my life, I believe a spirit came forth to protect me from being hit from any of the rounds.

#3 DESCENDING DEPTHS

In this life-threatening instance in the depths of Lake Huron, I experienced a whole new level of spiritual connection and found solace and love in the spirits who joined together to guide me through my transition into another realm and make it as easy and peaceful as possible. This experience was as close to enlightenment as I would ever get. During this time, I also learned about the greeter spirits who seemed to gently welcome individuals facing their same fate. They approached me gingerly and peacefully, welcoming me to my next phase of my spiritual journey. In hindsight, I felt like I was visiting an old friend at their own home, and when I returned I brought back knowledge of their history, story, feelings, emotions, experiences, and the traumatic events that led to their passing. Sadly, too, some spirits can be stuck between realms. I also became more instinctively self-confident about my own decisions and knew that I had to "keep moving forward" in this life.

#4 FLATLINE CHILDBIRTH

During this near-death experience, I crossed over twice while lying on the birthing bed during labour with my second child. The passage through the tunnel led me to my mother, and despite her telling me to go back, my spiritual body kept moving forward towards the gate of heaven, before I was pulled back to my physical body. The second time, shortly after this, I went past the gates and into heaven, saw the city and the people, saw the Angels before God, and Jesus preaching to his followers. The message that I brought back from this experience was to teach others several spiritual lessons. I could tell others that Heaven does exist, it is a peaceful and busy place, Jesus still teaches, and while we are there we will learn about our soul's journey, a part of us is living here on earth, but our higher self remains in Heaven to learn the lessons which we put into practice during our lives here on Earth.

#5 PHOENIX TRIP

As this story unfolds, you will see that our car flipped three and a half times. I survived, but had an enlightening, out-of-body experience during this. I learned early on that life could change within a flash of a moment—one moment you know where you have been, and you have a good idea of where you are going, until something untoward suddenly happens that puts you in a tailspin. Such an event occurred during my trip to Phoenix where I was forced to take a good look at my life and figure out the mess I was in. I found myself having to count on strangers to put all the pieces back together. This crisis sent me into a tailspin of emotions, forcing me to start my own healing process to rebuild my life. In order to "keep moving forward," it was imperative for me to handle this situation straight on with inner strength and courage.

#6 SHOCKING EXPERIENCE

I had another out of body experience when my children were very small and I was severely electrocuted. Although I had no feelings for my own physical body, I felt a tremendous amount for my own children, who were fast asleep two floors above me. There was no selfishness in my wish to remain alive; I prayed for my children's welfare. By the time I had mustered up enough strength to let go of the plug, it was revealed to me that all of us were in danger and it was all up to me not to give up. Sometimes even though it might seem impossible to let go of the things that are hurting us, letting go of what doesn't serve you can make all the difference in your life.

#7 PLUMETING ELEVATOR

The final turning point for me was an elevator accident on February 15th, 2002, in which I dropped 6 and a half floors at 125 km/hour and was left temporarily paralyzed. This came as a physical and spiritual blow as after years of effort, I had finally secured my dream job within the Federal Government, only to have it taken away by this accident. It took me over nine and a half years to recover but this experience helped me to finally see that I had been far off my true path in life. I'd been pursuing a career based on other people's approval, instead of pursuing a life that had deeper spiritual meaning and deeper relationships. While my other experiences had been about improving my relationships, this one had me lying in bed for two years straight thinking not about others, but about myself. Who was I, and why was I still living despite the seven accidents I had encountered? It was in this time that I finally figured it out: I was someone who had a purpose, and that purpose started with sharing my stories with others.

What I Hope You Will Take Away from My Story

If there is anything for you to take away from this book, it's "am I living a life that is worth living?" What is your true life purpose for being here, and how close are you to actually living a life that feels authentic to you?

If you've found yourself struggling through some tough situations, remember that we all have within us the personal strength to pull through, and to inspire others to do the same.

Please remember that this book is not meant to in any way replace professional guidance. I learned to heal from my painful past through years of counselling, spiritually connecting using mediumship, and from various support groups, organizations and churches. I had to learn to love and accept myself from the inside out.

It is my own opinion, through my own life experiences, that in order to heal from a traumatic experience, a person must involve all aspects of him or herself in order to truly heal from the inside out. It's a process that takes everything you have and everything you are. In order to reach your deepest inner feelings—physical, emotional and metaphysical—healing starts from the inside out, and it may consist of professional guidance, support groups, and family. This allows an awakening of transformation to begin.

1

SEEING GABRIEL

You can take the future even if you fail. I believe in angels, something good in everything I see.

—ABBA, *I Have a Dream*

The Story Begins

Shortly after my father Ted had returned home from his peacekeeping mission in Cyprus, when I was 6 months old, he left us for good. My mother's addiction to alcohol, and constant need to be the center of attention at the local bars and taverns, infuriated my father, and he left home within a few months. This left my mother alone to raise their five young children by herself, with only a babysitter to provide relief. Mom started to depend on my older siblings to take care of us, her youngest two daughters, me and my twin sister.

Eventually our older siblings' homework began to suffer, and as a result mom needed to find an alternative arrangement for her youngest twin daughters. By the time we reached two years old, we found ourselves constantly being shoved, hit and kicked back into our bedroom. I remember my mom laughing while closing our bedroom door behind us: "Out of sight, out of mind."

Over the next days, months and years, we were forced to spend our lives entirely behind our bedroom door. We were forced to remain quiet, and we learned to become ashamed of our very existence. Mom spent her time divided among her eldest three children, the bars, and entertaining men in our home (brought in after the nearby pubs had closed for the night), or being alone to soothe her wounds over a glass of gin and tonic. As my twin and I were forced to sit at the entrance of our bedroom door, we attempted to make a small enough slit between our door and its frame so we could see the outside world. We wanted to be able to see the rest of our family while they sat in the living room watching TV.

August 1971

Mom received a letter from the Board of Education. It stated that my twin and I had to start kindergarten, as we had reached four years of age. We had been left alone in our bedroom for the past two years, but now she was being forced to unify us with our peers in a structured environment, to attend school with the rest of the kids our age. This was the first time we realized that not only was our treatment different than our siblings, but our situation was completely unique compared to all of our classmates. The daily taunting, and emotional and physical abuse that we received from the hands of our mother was infuriating and inhuman. It broke our hearts when we realized that we were alone to face our mother's abusive behaviour as she continued to lock us in our room on a nightly basis, despite us having started school.

It didn't take long before our teacher recognized that we had behaviour issues, identified us as troubled youth, and left us to our own devices. She reported that we were unusually quiet, timid, introverted, and had no recognizable language, but she assumed that we would eventually develop in a special education program.

However, we continued to fall further behind the rest of the students in our classrooms, as we had to repeat both grades one and two. We had to start speech therapy, which forced us to be separated in order to encourage us to start communicating with other children our age. Heidi took it upon herself to speak to her own teacher in hopes of resolving some of our issues at home. However, this backfired when her teacher promptly approached the situation with our mother. Mom was livid. When we got picked up by both our brother and mom at the end of that same day, I knew I was in trouble. She leaned over the front seat, slapped me across the face and said, "Tonight just wait until you get home; you're getting the double-dose." We came to recognize that each time we received the double-dose it meant that she was doubling our previous beating. That particular beating was so severe that both Heidi and I promised each other never to tell another adult; we kept our promise for five years.

When our older siblings finished elementary school and they began leaving home early, Mom's abusive nature escalated. She became incredibly defensive of her financial situation and began counting all of the items in our cupboards, fridge, and pantry, and declared the kitchen off limits for both Heidi and me. She stated that if anything was taken from the kitchen, it would be classified as stealing, and she would punish us according to the ancient Catholic standards. We had heard from a priest the old phrase "Spare the rod, spoil the child." Mom believed that it meant that she was to enforce strict punishment on us.

We had to stay away from the food in our home, or we could count on being beaten. On the one hand, the Catholic school's priest told me that my spirit would go to hell if I stole anything. On the other hand, my teacher informed me that I had to bring at least a sandwich in my lunch box every day, or mom would be called. To us, that meant another reason for mom to spank us in order to keep us in line. Our teacher stated that she had no choice, as her hands were tied, and that the school's principal would have to call our mother to come into the office to explain why we didn't have anything in our lunch boxes.

When we sat around the table with the rest of the kids for lunch, it was truly embarrassing. The table monitor always watched me closely to see what I brought to school. Initially, I had brought the exact same sandwich in my lunch box on a daily basis. I would take a tiny bite every day until the sandwich grew mould and I could no longer eat it. Next, I survived on scraps of food that Heidi and I scavenged after our mother's parties with strangers. Food was left on the various surfaces around our home. However, one day my mother found it in my lunch box and beat me for stealing, putting an end to that endeavour.

Eventually, I started acting like the Lost Boys in a story I recently heard called *Peter Pan: The Boy Who Never Grew Up*. Peter, along with his friends, created a magical feast and pretended to eat imaginary food that appeared on their large table in front of them. In my case, it was just a sandwich in my lunch box.

One day, during lunch in grade 3, the table monitor bestowed a disgusting look towards me. The monitor stated to the teacher, "Madame, Holly's acting crazy again, pretending she has a lunch when we all can see that her lunch box is empty. She is also bothering the kids at our table for their lunch." I sat there ashamed, trying to hold back my tears, being brave and yet worried how mom would react if she found out. The teacher stormed over and stood over top of me yelling, "Stop bothering the other kids," and instructed me to go sit with my eyes to the corner inside the closet. I stood in the coat closet, as instructed, where I learned how to cry quietly to myself in order to avoid more taunting during recesses by the other kids in the playground.

The Loaded Stick

Over the next couple of years, we lived in three different residences around London, Ontario. No matter where we lived, Mom always displayed the Irish Shillelagh Stick that she had received from one of her family members back home in Ireland. She left the stick in a prominent location within our home, for everyone to see on a regular basis. It reminded her of family, friends, and her homeland. It offered guests a conversational piece they could focus on, placing mom at the center of attention.

I remember several times when she took the Shillelagh Stick off the wall and proceeded to hit me with it. Shillelagh Sticks are made from blackthorn wood root or oak, unlike the wooden spoons she had used on both my twin and me many times. This wooden stick was made strong and less likely to crack during use. Its 'hitting end' was filled with lead, giving its nickname of 'the loaded stick.' There was a strap to place around the user's wrist to secure it.

The stick hung on our living room wall beside other picture framed centrepieces. I remember the four-leaf clovers on its tip. The clovers intrigued all her guests. The stick was a constant reminder to my twin and me of just how much our lives were lived in a twisted balance, between what others saw and what we experienced. As soon as her guests would leave, she would turn a wonderful piece of artwork into a weapon against us. Being young, I was under the impression that my mother's family, back in Ireland, completely supported her decision to use it against us, despite the fact that they didn't even know us. She continued year after year to create more bruises, as they formed layer over layer.

Mom's resentment towards us increased over the years as her abusive temper grew, until one night, when I was 11 years old, she arrived home from work with a headache and a very low tolerance for noise. She instructed her three youngest children, who shared her bedroom, to go to bed early and be quiet. Despite mom's constant warnings to my two sisters, they continued to play. This frustrated and angered mom immensely. I begged them to stop but they wouldn't. Before long, mom lost her temper. She came charging, swung open the bedroom door and stomped over to Heidi's and my bunk beds. Ignoring my sisters, she proceeded to pull me off the top bunk by my long hair.

I noticed mom's face right away; it was full of rage and hatred. I begged her to let me go—that it hadn't been me. She said it didn't matter, and that I was getting it anyways. She flung me out of the top bunk and thumped my side onto the floor. She grabbed my pyjama collar like a rope with which to drag me. She dragged me past the Shillelagh Stick hanging on our wall in our living room. She pulled it off the wall, then dragged me into the kitchen, and flung me around like a little rag doll. I hit every appliance.

I attempted to fight her off while I pleaded with her to let me go. She wouldn't stop, and became even more aggressive every time I spoke.

After ten minutes of her hitting me with her rolling pin, pots, pans, and Shillelagh Stick, I was completely drained. Both my physical body and spirit felt totally empty. Every part of my body had enormous amounts of alarming pain shooting through it from every direction. I lay there in a weakened state, praying for my life. She had beaten me so badly that I started to lose my zest for life.

Recollecting my senses, I aimed to regain a false sense of calmness. I hoped that she would stop and permit me to go back to my bed so I could lie in my bed and die in peace. The years of torture, beatings and lost hope had taken a toll on me, and I didn't care anymore. Finally, when she noticed that I had given up the fight, the beating was over (or so I thought); she no longer needed to get her frustrations out. She ordered me to go to bed but my body had finally failed to move. I had no strength left, having just received the worst beating of my life.

Mom grabbed the back of my pyjama collar, lifted me off my feet and threw me a couple of feet towards the bedroom door. I landed hard against the floor. She picked me up and dropped me another two feet off the ground. As I hit the floor, she bellowed out, "You're not moving fast enough!" Mom hit me again, grabbed my collar and threw me closer to the bedroom. As I recaptured my balance, I tried to crawl forward but she grabbed my collar and threw me for a third time. I began to wonder where God was during all this.

I looked up at the person who I had come to know as my mom. I recognized a dark shadow doubling her size standing in her place, as though it wasn't even my mother who was standing over me. Confused, but even more scared, I made an instant declaration not to allow her or this entity to destroy my full potential as an individual. I refused to carry her burden, or share her darkness, or inflict pain on another person, like she had done on Heidi and me.

She continued to pick me up **and** throw me another couple of feet, again and again on the surface of the floor hard. Once, I had landed with my face staring right at her, but I was unprepared to face my perpetrator straight on. As I had lain there looking at her, she kicked me directly in my face, causing my neck to crack. Without any regard for my well-being, she continued to beat me, punching and hauling me the next couple of feet, as she yelled out the hurtful words that I had heard many times before: "You're stupid, retarded, ugly; and I hate you!" Excruciating, inflamed joints ached as I tried to crawl on my hands and knees. I was determined to make the journey to our bedroom. As I reached the bedroom, my mother ordered my sisters out of bed so they could assist me in getting back onto the top bunk. They jumped out of bed and complied, as if they heard nothing; they had pretended to be asleep throughout the ordeal. They thrust me into the top bunk from the ladder at the end of my bed. I slithered onto my pillow, where I lay down my head. Mom yelled, "Now you kids better get some sleep, or I will come back in here and get somebody else next time!" Heidi was scared, as she knew that she would be mom's next victim, so she told me to be quiet and go to sleep.

Seeing Gabriel

I settled down and sobbed under my pillow. I wished my sisters had listened to me when I told them to be quiet earlier. Heidi pronouncedly whispered, "Stop crying. I don't want mom to come here again." I positioned my head under my pillow and wept quietly so nobody could hear me. I prayed for God to carry me home. I prayed with all my energy, "God have mercy on my soul," as these words rounded off my heart in prayer:

"God in heaven please pray for me. Please bring me a sign that I'm going to live past tonight. I need to know if this is the place I am supposed to be, or should you let me go, please let me know. I need to know if you want to take me home.

"Please, I don't want to live, anymore!

"I hope you can understand me, but I can't see how I can continue in a world that hates me so much. I know you died on the cross for the sins of the world, but I ask you what sins I have done to deserve so much. Have I forsaken you? Have you deserted me? Am I not worthy of your love? Have I not served you right, my Lord? If there is no other purpose for me in this life, if this all that I have come here for, if this is it then, please take me home now. You have the power to take away the sins of the world; why did you leave me here in so much pain?

"Why do I have to suffer so much? They say, Lord, that you only give us as much as we can handle, but I have already handled enough, and I am tired. I will do whatever you want me to do, but if this is the only reason why I am here, please take me home, as I have served my purpose and beg you to release me from all this pain. Show me a sign that I will make it to adulthood, or deliver me from this kingdom of darkness and evil that surrounds me now. I am your servant, I will obey, but I need a little strength to carry me forward in my days.

"Please Lord, have mercy on my soul and show me a sign that you want me to continue to serve you, or take me out of this place tonight."

With that I must have collapsed into a dreamlike state. When I awoke a few hours later, I saw an angel floating near the end of my bunk bed. As he floated above the ground, his beautiful bright face lit up the whole room and his enormous wings draped over his shoulders. I began to switch back and forth between my physical and spiritual bodies. I opened and closed my eyes repeatedly and shook my head while I was in my physical form to see if the glimpse of the angel disappeared, testing if the figure had been of my imagination. Gabriel remained steadfast at the end of my bed.

He lingered in peaceful tranquility, waiting for me to absorb his entire being in my physical, mental, emotional and spiritual realms. As I kept flashing back and forth between the dimensions, Gabriel remained patient with me, as if to teach me that I had a choice of where I wanted to exist. It was as though my higher power was giving me an opportunity to decide between the different dimensions, or paths. He was showing me that I had the choice to live in this physical realm.

A few seconds later, I realized that it was my spiritual form in which I needed to stay in order to be able to listen to my spiritual teacher speak. His silhouette hovered in front of me as an incredible amount of peace came over me. I became lightweight, filled with a feeling of an abundance of the love that Gabriel brought me. He gave me a message that God had not forsaken me!

Prosperous love, harmony, and an impression of belonging overwhelmed me. Gabriel came in with the most peaceful light that was also blinding. His complexion became distinctively, indeterminately transparent, as he gave me time to decide my spiritual journey; to have me reflect about my decision to come down to earth. I knew that I, like everyone else, had been given an opportunity before arriving here, to decide what my life path would be and its purpose. Gabriel wanted me to remember that, although it was unconventional, this path was one of my own choosing.

Gabriel wanted me to remember this precise moment for the rest of my life. I could look upon this moment whenever I felt that I was totally afraid and suffering; I was not alone. I regained my spiritual form for the final time. Watching intently, Gabriel smiled at me and slowly spread his wings wide. He spoke in a telepathic manner to me without moving his mouth and transferred a magnificent and harmonious message in his angelic voice:

"My dearest child, you are not alone! Tell everyone that we have not forgotten them. We hear your prayers. We are right here beside you, watching over you.

"The pain you feel is not your own; but it has been chosen for you. Whenever you need us, just pray and we will be there to be your guiding light. Although you chose to come here, you are not alone, we have not abandoned you.

"You have come here to teach others that this work you do is not in vain. You have been called upon to restore faith in the Holy Spirit."

As he spoke, the angel extended his arms and revealed four children. They stood in front of him by his bosom, guarded under his wings. Both the oldest and youngest of the children were girls. They stood on either side of another girl with a young boy, who would be her son, standing in front of her. I was told telepathically to call the middle girl Jaccinta-Marie, and that she would be born with many physical challenges and bring many trials and tribulations into my life. Gabriel wanted me to focus on the male child; he would be significant in my life and the lives of those he met during his journey.

Once the message was delivered, Gabriel disappeared as instantaneously as he had come. I rebounded back to my physical body and in the morning I discussed my experience with my twin sister. I felt enormous hope and faith that we would make it through, despite growing up under my mother's roof; that her abuse would not last. I would indeed make it to adulthood. Even though the spirits allowed me to make the final decision, they wanted me to know that my life would be difficult, but worth living for the growth of my spiritual, higher self.

The Bamboo Slivers

Late one night, when I was 12, shortly after she got remarried to a man by the name of Narse, mom came home in a panic. The two of them had been in an argument at the restaurant where they worked. Throughout the evening they had been drinking in the adjacent tavern. She came home terrified that Narse was going to kill her. She told us, "I am going back out. If you see Narse do not tell him anything. The only thing you are allowed to say to him is that I have gone out."

When we saw him, we answered in the manner in which mom had instructed. This infuriated him. He yelled "Yes, I know that, but where?" We couldn't answer that question. We had pleaded with our mother to tell us more. She refused. He left our bedroom only to return a few seconds later. He returned with a bamboo stick, a decoration from our living room. He immediately started hitting us fiercely **with it** until it broke over my head. Grabbing the longer piece off the floor, he walked over to Heidi and broke it over her body. He threw the broken sticks down on the floor and stormed out of our home in search of our mother.

The next morning, we saw our sister Theresa in the bathroom. She firmly told us to stop crying like babies: "You're always crying like babies, what is up with you?" We tried to explain to her that the times we cried like babies were in direct correlation to the nightly beatings we received. She just rolled her eyes and said

"I don't know what you're talking about. Narse didn't come into my room. In fact, I slept like a baby all night long," she laughed, and walked out of the bathroom. "Now get ready for school or I will tell our mother that you two interfered with my school and you'll be in big trouble!"

We were left standing in the bathroom. I asked Heidi how we were going to conceal this beating. She said there was no way to hide it, and that we needed medical help. It was true, the embedded bamboo slivers were burning like cyanide poisoning, causing immense pain. Heidi was afraid that we needed medical treatment right away or the slivers would get badly infected, potentially causing death.

That morning, my class went to St. Robert's School for the Deaf for our regular swimming class. I waited patiently for the other girls to change in the dressing room before changing myself. I remained quiet, not confiding in any of the girls in my class, as I lived in fear of mom's double-dose beatings. While the rest of my classmates were out swimming, my teacher counted heads and noticed that I was missing from the pool. She came bursting into the change room and with a firm voice demanded, "Holly, come out or I am going to call your mother." Immediately, my teacher noticed that my face was red, as I had been crying, and told me to walk over to the sink and wash up. As I leaned over and turned on the taps, she noticed the twenty or more bamboo slivers embedded in my back. She grew very upset and demanded an answer: "Who did this to you?"

She immediately instructed the spare teacher, who had accompanied her into the change room, to go to the door and ask one of the life guards to fetch the medical staff. As two other adults were in the bathroom with me, my teacher promptly dismissed herself to call our school. A few minutes later she returned stating "Your sister is sitting in the office right now. When we arrive back at the school, you are to come with me to the principal's office. A CAS [Children's Aid Society] worker, along with the the school Principal, Vice-Principals, and Counsellor are in the office with your twin. They want to speak to you in detail about this bamboo incident and your family issues."

A New Hope

For the entire time we sat in the office, the Principal repeated, "You are safe, we are all here listening to you, and we all have powerful positions. We can stop the abuse if you open up and tell us, and we are going to protect you. I promise the abuse is over."

While pointing to the various people in the room, he introduced me to the Children's Aid Society (CAS) representative present there and to other representatives who I knew from the hallways at school. None of them knew our full story. I waited quietly as I held Heidi's hand. How could we be safe? Nobody had stopped her beatings before. Now these people wanted us to feel completely comfortable about disclosing the many years of abuse. Remembering years earlier when the double dose started, we learned never to reveal our home life to anyone.

I started to share and burst into tears, letting go of years of pain. I felt relieved. I was crying so hard I could barely breathe. I finally let go of all the tension I had held inside during all the years of abuse, neglect, near starvation, nightly beatings, and isolation by being locked inside of our room. Now everything came down to this moment. My eyes filled with tears, my arms and legs began to shake as I let go of all the pressure inside and began to cry openly. The representatives listened intensely to our childhood history and for the first time in my life, I finally felt completely safe.

After a few minutes of intense sharing, the principal exclaimed that he had to call our mother at work. My heart dropped right through the floor, and I thought, oh no! My heart began to beat harder, I could barely breathe, and my palms were sweating. I felt like we had been double-crossed by these people and immediately tensed up again. I feared that our now told secrets were going to get us into a lot more trouble. Our safe haven was gone! My knees began to shake when I heard my mother answer the phone and my principal began to speak to her about our conversation:

"Mrs. Kline, this is the principal at your daughter's school. I have both Heidi and Holly in our office right now; they are sitting right here in front of me. Now, I want you to know that we also have the CAS, and School Counsellor in my office with us.

"Mrs. Kline, both Heidi and Holly have been discussing in detail the years of abuse that they have been suffering under your roof. These incidents include a very recent incident with a bamboo stick that included your husband, Narse, for which we have extensive evidence. Although we will be sending them home to you tonight, if you lay one finger on them, we will be arresting you immediately for child abuse and neglect, and you will be going to jail for a long, long time. Do you understand me?"

I heard my mother saying, "Yes, I do." Through her immediate response and the tension in her voice, I knew that she would be angry when she hung up the phone.

I immediately tensed back up, and didn't want to talk to anyone. At the end of the day when we walked home, I worried how much of the double dose we were going to get that night. However, we were pleasantly shocked when the beating never came. We knew something was up as she asked our brother over to our home for dinner and Heidi and I to join the family at the dinner table. At first, I felt the conversation at school had actually worked, and that she finally had to be nice to us, but I wondered how long that was going to last. At the end of the meal, mom opened with a family discussion about the phone call she had received at work that day from our principal. She said as a result, she and Narse had decided to move out to another province and asked us if we wanted to come with her. I bravely declined, knowing the beatings would restart in her new home.

She gave us three choices: we could either live with her, our brother, or our Dad. Heidi and I felt we had no choice but to live with our Dad. Our mother had repeatedly called our brother, who was eight years our elder, to come into our house to hit us whenever she felt we needed to be "put back in line."

All week we wondered when we were going to be beaten, but instead she just continued to send us to our bedroom, while she repeatedly played two songs on eight-track, such as John Denver's *Leaving on a Jet Plane* and Anne Murray's *Snowbird*, which were intermingled with other songs from the radio.

We were surprised Friday morning when both our mother and Theresa sent us off to school that morning. We knew something was up because our mother was staying home to take care of a supposedly sick Theresa, but Theresa had been acting fine all morning and our mother never stayed home with her sick children. When we arrived home after school, we tried to open our front door, but couldn't. Dumped on the cement platform of the veranda were two garbage bags labelled with our names carefully written. We stood on our tippy-toes and strenuously looked through the window into our living room. Everything was gone. The only items left were our garbage bags full of clothes. The words in the two songs came flooding in our minds as well as mom's past threats, "Be good or I will throw you out with the garbage." It wasn't until this moment that we realized she meant it.

Above the garbage bags, there was a small note taped to our front door. Our hearts sank as we read her note, "I've moved out west. Call your Dad. Here is his contact information, Master Corporal Kline—Mom." With that, we walked across the parking lot to our next door neighbour's and asked the family if we could use their phone. However, the man noticed we were having a hard time dialling. As his wife offered to console us, the husband dialled the number listed on the paper. We were barely able to stand as all of our emotions came rushing to the surface, so we held on tightly to each other. We felt totally devastated knowing that our mom had abandoned us for the last time, leaving us totally alone. This made us realize that no matter what we did to please her over the years, she never loved us back. Dad answered the phone and told us that he was on his way and would leave work immediately. He picked us up and brought us over to his house, where we took up residence with his new wife Bonnie, and our two stepsisters Brenda and Beatrice.

Stairway to Heaven
By the time I was 16, after a few years of adjusting to our new lifestyle under our Dad's roof with our new family, Heidi and I both decided to fly out to Calgary to visit our mother. She had sent us constant requests to visit her, as she had recently been diagnosed with cancer and didn't know how long she would live. Heidi and I coordinated our visits. Heidi visited Mom for a week. The evening Heidi was due to fly home I arrived before her departure with several hours to spare. Our mother took us to the local tavern for a bite to eat and to listen to the local band playing. The band asked the audience if there were any songs that they wanted dedicated to another patron.

I walked gingerly over to the band and asked them to dedicate the song "Led Zeppelin, *Stairway to Heaven*" to my mother. The band asked me to explain to the audience why I had chosen that particular song. I stated that I had just arrived from London, Ontario, as my mother had been recently diagnosed with cancer and didn't know how long she would live and I wanted her to know that when she crosses, I hoped that she would find her staircase to heaven. Some women in the bar began to cry, including our mother. As the band began playing, I returned to our table.

Mom sat there, listening carefully to the lyrics of the song. Our mother reached out her hand to us in a gentle manner and asked for our forgiveness for the years of torment that she had put us through.

Hesitation set in because the fear of her was still alive, but both Heidi and I gracefully gave her our forgiveness as the band played the song. I thanked her for being my mother and for bringing me into this world. I told her that I understood that her life had been difficult and even though I had suffered through too many of the blunt teachings, I always loved her. I explained that the true forgiveness that she was seeking was through the Holy Spirit and that she still had some time to turn her life around. I personally wished her well and hoped that she would reach "the stairway to heaven" when it came for her time to leave.

She thanked me for being so understanding of all those years, for providing her insights into the Holy Spirit, for my love, the song, and my prayers.

I heard later that once Heidi and I left Calgary, mom separated from her husband Narse and moved into a homeless shelter, where she served for many years as **their** cook as she offered the children emotional support. She created a bond with their clients, as she intently listened to the families' abusive stories, and learned about their pain. She later told me that she regretted that she had never been there for us, her own children, and that if she could go back, she would have done things differently. She said she never forgot the moment we had in the tavern.

2

DOWN RANGE

The true soldier fights not because he hates what is in front of him, but because he loves what he left behind.
—G.K. CHESTERTON

A New Life

Learning to live in a new family, away from mom while she got on with her life out West, was very difficult. I missed her and thought about her often, and wondered if she ever thought about me. I tried not to let it interfere with my own life, but by the time I was 14, I had already been in conflicts with my Dad's new family and started living a swinging-door life style. I had a Cinderella stepfamily as I was living on and off the streets since his wife Bonnie would change her mind about me living with them.

Despite this challenging situation at home, I excelled during my teenage years. I served as a member of #9 Royal Canadian Army Cadets, achieving the rank of Corporal with a Silver Star and Wreath level. I was crowned Queen of my high school in grade 9, was voted in by my fellow student politicians to the position of Mayor of Youth in Student Government for the City of London, sponsored by the Optimist Club. I obtained the Silver Duke of Edinburgh Award by my Cadet Corp, and I was voted the most likely to succeed in High School by the teachers and students.

At age 17, with my Dad's signature, I relinquished my position in the #9 Royal Canadian Army Cadets to move on to something greater. It was a bittersweet time for me. I had to leave my former friends, the only attachments I had since moving in with Dad over three years earlier. However, I was looking forward to implementing my years of volunteer experience as a cadet into my new paid position with the 22nd Service Battalion, located at the 19 Becker Street Armouries, London, Ontario.

That summer was gruelling and incredibly draining as I built up my physical fitness as a soldier. When we arrived for the first day of training, Sergeant Finch, my commanding officer, ordered us to "fall-in" immediately. The experienced soldiers started to form a platoon formation. While standing at attention, one of the experienced soldiers called out, "Hey you, newbie, come stand over here. Yeah that's right, you, stand there." This soldier pointed to an empty spot on the concrete floor among the other soldiers. From our sergeant's vantage point, it was easy to pick out the new recruits with previous military training versus those with none. While the new soldiers didn't understand the command and looked completely lost, the rest of us formed three lines deep, standing arm distance away from each other.

Our sergeant strictly announced, "Only one third of you will make it to the end of the course. Those of you who make it need to know that you can count on each other in order to survive the training, as well as whatever you may face in your military career. You need to be able to trust, honour, and support each other. He or she may be the only person you have to depend on with your very lives. The standards we are expecting will test you physically, mentally, and emotionally in order to prepare you for anything that you may face in your career within the Canadian Forces. You will be taught and expected to know various aspects of military life from your dress, deportment, physical endurance, Canadian Military History, and your Battalion's History and Colors." He continued, "We will travel to various places around Ontario for the more extensive training, and each base is specific for each part of your training. This nine-week basic training will be held in: Meaford, Borden, Kingston, and Ipperwash. Do you understand what I have told you?" We answered "Yes, Sergeant," and with that he stated "Your basic training starts now. Get down and give me twenty."

During our training in Meaford, we faced simulated survival training in the forest. While at Borden, we learned rock climbing and rappelling. We went into Kingston's gas chambers, which were commonly referred to as the puke patrol. There, with a mask on, we did our predefined exercise and at the end, while still inside, we had to take off our mask, give our rank, surname, and social insurance number to our sergeant before we could leave. At Ipperwash, we did a physical obstacle course and target practice. Although Meaford and Borden were far more naturally beautiful, CFB Ipperwash was my favourite.

CFB Ipperwash is located in Lambton County, near Kettle Point, Ontario. It was among my favourite bases as it brought back memories of my own cadet camp experiences. While sitting on the yellow bus with my comrades, I remained quiet, listening to everyone on the bus making various comments about the base. As I sat there listening, I stared out my window reminiscing about the previous years, the people I had met, and some of my courses and experiences. A fellow comrade, Brian, asked me what I was looking for out my window, as he noticed that I was obviously excited. I informed him that this was my army cadet base and that I had years of experience and extensive knowledge about the camp itself. He replied "Yea, like what?"

I informed him that in April 1942, the Department of National Defense (DND) acquired the land from the Chippewas of Kettle and Stoney Point First Nations during the middle of WWII when the DND imposed the War Measures Act, expropriating the property. Pointing out my window to where the bus had used a wide space to drive onto the parade square, I mentioned that all these barracks and the firing range, which were way past all the buildings, were built in 1942. This base was used for the infantry "boot camp" to train Canadian soldiers before heading overseas for World War II. Once the war was completed, the province was thinking of handing parts of the base back to the Kettle and Stoney Point First Nations, but they wanted all or nothing so they refused the offer. So we kept the base as a training facility for both the regular forces, reserves and the Cadet summer training camp. This included my former unit—the #9 Royal Canadian Regiment—and all of the other Royal Canadian Army Cadets who began their cadet training in 1948. I then let him know that twenty years ago there was another men's barracks making a complete circle around the parade square, but a young boy was playing with matches and the whole barracks burned down to the ground in less than four minutes.

I continued to tell him that we almost lost the base in 1972, when the Minister of Indian Affairs stated the land claim for the expropriation was valid. However, DND still did not relinquish control. The land remained in the hands of DND from 1970s onwards, as Ipperwash was still used as a firing range training facility for all the soldiers and for the provincial police.

The bus driver opened the door and we started to pile off the bus and onto the parade square. Brian thanked me for informing him about the history of the base. We piled our kits outside of the bus, into one giant pile. We then formed into our platoon and were told that we would not be sleeping in the barracks. Instead we would simulate being dropped into unknown enemy territory. We had to work simultaneously with other units and forces that we didn't know, but who were our allies. At the end of the weekend we would be given an extra hour in which to properly clean our rifles and have them inspected by our section leaders. As the last part of the maneuvers, we were to fire our FN-C2-A1 7.62MM firearms on the firing range with twenty live rounds on semi-automatic bursts. Once we were all formed into our platoon, we picked up our nylon covered kit bags and followed our sergeant out to the forest area to pitch our tents. We were wearing our standard olive-drab combats and black combat boots while carrying our FN-C2 rifles. Once we had walked several miles into the forest behind the barracks, we were told to set up tent and started our first of several two-hour sleep cycles, before our next checkpoint several miles away.

In the last phase of our sleep deprivation exercise, our sergeant granted us an extra couple of hours of sleep, and a half hour to clean our firearms before we marched the last quarter mile to the firing range. I began to wonder which one of the distance firing mounts we would be using. As I was not a marksman and was sleep deprived, I was concerned about my firing grouping, and that I might not pass my basic if my aim on the target was off.

Sergeant Finch informed me that we would be shooting from 500 meters, but the aim of the weekend exercise was based more on the ability to do the entire exercise and not on the grouping specifically, as we had plenty of time during our military careers to improve our targeting skills.

The Rules

Sergeant Finch was personally responsible for all personnel and for strictly enforcing safety protocols during target practice. Making sure everybody listened, the sergeant went over all the rules:

1. Always put your firearm down-range under every and any condition;

2. Should the firearm jam, remain calm and follow step one;

3. Should an emergency occur, continue to point your firearm down-range and turn on the safety;

4. Put your arm up in the air and an RO (Range Officer) Assistant will come over to you to assist with any problems;

5. Wait patiently.

He expressed how vitally important it was to keep our firearms down-range, as the previous year a soldier was killed instantly when a comrade beside him had his firearm jam. He hadn't followed the rule of keeping the firearm pointed down-range. Consequently, when he swung his rifle towards his comrade, the firearm went off, emptying all twenty rounds into his friend's torso, cutting him completely in half. Our sergeant finished by stating that anyone caught waving their firearm in a way that can and/or does injure another soldier would be immediately escorted from the firing range by the Military Police (MP), and would receive a dishonourable discharge and two years in Edmonton Military Jail, or a combination of jail and two years of Community Service.

We had to attest to the sergeant that we understood his rules, regulations and consequences of disobeying those rules, by all saying, "Yes, Sergeant." Once we were cleared for firing, we took our firearms up to the firing range mount—a pack of dirt standing approximately three feet higher than where we had presently been standing. Our sergeant had a great view of every soldier on the firing range, as he remained behind us and overlooked the entire section.

Hearing the news that a fellow soldier unfortunately had been killed last year, I was extremely alert of my fellow comrades who were also firing. We were given the command, "Begin firing at your own leisure," which meant when the soldier had his firearm in the proper position, he could begin firing at the target in front of him.

After taking a few shots, I noticed Private Frank out of the corner of my eye. He stood to my immediate left, as I stood on the far right, in the last position on the firing range. He looked like he was panicking, as his rifle had malfunctioned. He had disengaged several live rounds, as he had pulled his trigger several times after the first round jammed in his rifle. Being an experienced soldier, I realized that he was in more severe situation than he even realized. Once that first round disengaged from whatever was holding it in his firearm, all the rounds that he had pulled the trigger to release would quickly release right behind it. However, he kept pulling the trigger, hitting the barrel, and swinging his rifle around with no regard to where his firearm was pointing.

Frank started to point the chamber of his firearm up towards the sky and then twisted it around to face him. Disregarding the sergeant's commands, he changed the position of his rifle to point towards his own face.

I yelled at him, "Hey, Frank I wouldn't do that if I were you. That's live and you never know when that is going to go off!"

He responded by saying, "You are right!" as he changed the direction of his firearm, again.

I told him to stop pulling the trigger, but he wasn't listening to me. He just continued pulling, releasing more bullets jamming behind the first round, and waving his firearm. By now he had a fully automatic firearm, which terrified me as I watched him become irrational and start to panic. I quickly put my own firearm on safety, put it on the ground, keeping my barrel of my firearm pointed down-range.

Standing in shock, I noticed Private Frank start to slowly turn his rifle towards me. I couldn't believe the nerve of this soldier. I had just possibly saved his life and now he was starting to turn his fully automatic machine rifle at me.

A Barrage of Bullets

Frank slapped both the barrel and magazine again. The first projectile discharged less than a foot away from my head. Suddenly, I felt someone push me from behind causing me to fall, and I hit my face on the ground right in front of where I had been standing. Just then, a round whooshed right through the spot I had just been standing. The next bullet landed about four inches from the right side of my face, as Frank had lowered his rifle.

The rest of the cartridges started automatically discharging. With each blast coming closer to me, I was in shock, frozen still, as live projectiles flew less than a few inches away from my body. In fear of being killed, I lay there defensively and couldn't wait for this terror to be finished, praying, "God, please, protect me." I prayed that his shot would miss!

Frank was not focusing on the direction of his firearm's chamber. Rather, he was more concerned about finding the safety clip and turning it on. He seemed totally clueless that all his live rounds were barely missing my body. Lying on the ground, I heard the bullets continue to land around my body.

I lay there defenseless. All I had was my helmet and combats to protect me. Had the live bullets hit any one of my vital organs, I would have been instantly dead and my sergeant would be removing another deceased body from his firing range. I lay there helpless. One bullet hit less than a foot from my head while others seemed to land as though they had grazed my tunic. The bullets that hit near me dug into the ground, sending puffs of dirt all over my combats. I continued to pray that this was not my time to go. My heart clenched with terror at the sound of bullets coming out of his chamber.

I remained on the ground with my hands over my helmet. I realized that Frank's firearm was finally empty. I paused for a few seconds. I thanked the Holy Spirit for keeping me alive, as I continued to lie on the ground on my torso. By the time his magazine had emptied twenty live rounds, a layer of dirt was totally covering me and one of the hot bullet carriages had landed on the middle of my back while all the others landed around the circumference of my body.

I was in shock, but ecstatic that none of the bullets had hit me. On the other hand, I was completely pissed that Frank seemed to be totally oblivious to what had just taken place. His attention was solely on his own firearm and he looked proud that he had found the safety, stating, "Oh, so that is where the safety switch is!"

Sergeant Finch called an immediate, "Cease Fire!" He then ordered, "Raise the Cease-Fire flags and fall in!"

The soldier on the opposite side of my firing position followed his command, put his firearm on the ground, raised the firing flag and replaced it with the cease-fire flag. It meant that our platoon was finished firing and that it was safe for the men in the bunkers of the target range to return to the front lines.

As the rest of us soldiers stood beside our firearms in the at-ease position, waiting patiently for the RSO firing range officer to call, "Fall In," I noticed just how many live bullet cartridges were around where I had just been lying.

In a state of shock, I physically scanned my whole body to make sure that I had not been grazed by any of the bullets. Sergeant Finch was frustrated that another soldier had almost died due to friendly fire under his command. He spoke with a very caring concern for my personal well being, asking, "Private Kline, how are you? Are you okay?"

"Yes Sergeant, I am fine; a little shaken up by the whole ordeal. I wasn't shot, so I will be fine."

I didn't want to show any signs of weakness in order to sustain my high standard of macho attitude for being a female soldier, in a man's army. I had just one question, "Where did the soldier go who pushed me down at the specific second that I was being fired at? Did you see him? I want to thank him for saving my life."

Sergeant Finch turned to me and answered, "I saw the entire thing. I even saw what looked like you being pushed from behind, but there was no soldier in your area at the time. However, it did very much look like you had been pushed from behind, the way you fell so quickly and suddenly, but there was no one there."

Sergeant Finch next said, "It is perfectly understandable to be shaken up. I saw the entire incident. I have called the Military Police. They are on their way to arrest him. They will deal with him firmly. Don't you worry, I have your back."

Just then Private Frank joined the rest of us in the Platoon formation. He asked who were coming and why, as he had caught the end of Sergeant Finch's and my conversation. He started to protest, stating they didn't need to come as he was just putting his firearm on safety and no one got hurt.

The sergeant responded with a finger pointed at Frank, "Take the shoelaces out of your shoes!"

Sergeant Finch waited for Frank's shoelaces and placed them into my hand. Private Frank very reluctantly asked, "Why do I have to take my shoelaces out of my boots?" The sergeant responded, "It's the standard operational procedure to have a soldier remove his shoelaces from his boots when he is being arrested."

Within a few minutes, two MPs arrived shortly after Finch got Frank's shoelaces. They parked their jeep on the road, climbed out and walked over to our platoon. Reporting to our sergeant, they asked, "What seems to be the problem here?"

Sergeant Finch pointed at Frank. "Arrest this private for misconduct of a live firearm!" He went into an explanation of the whole ordeal in front of the whole platoon. Now, with everybody paying attention to both Private Frank and myself, the rest of the soldiers in the platoon where totally shocked that I was taking it so easily, and started to rub my shoulders and give me support.

The two MPs walked over to either side of Private Frank, read him his charges and gave him his rights, then put handcuffs on him and marched him over to the jeep where they loaded him into their vehicle. They told the sergeant to come with me to their office to make a full report.

Sergeant Finch asked me if I wanted to go to a counsellor or remain with the platoon. I immediately responded, I want to remain with the platoon. We marched back into camp while everybody else was dismissed, and both my sergeant and I walked over to the MP's office and made a formal report.

I graduated basic training on August 27th, 1984, three months before my 18th birthday.

Every day, I am grateful for having served my country, and I give a little thank you prayer for the spirit who helped me during my basic training. As I had been standing virtually on the same spot as the soldier who had been killed the previous year, the nearest I can figure is that it was his spirit that had pushed me out of the way of the live rounds, as he probably didn't want to see any soldier face his fate.

3

DESCENDING DEPTHS

Find me here Lord as you draw me near.
—*HILLSONG, Cornerstone*

Home For Summer

At the end of August of 1984, after basic training, Dad drove me up to Ipperwash to be with my twin sister and stepfamily. Our family had a lot of campsite seasonal closing chores up in Ipperwash to be completed before school started the following week. Dad refused to allow me to linger in the house, as he had stated I would be lazy watching TV all day while he went to work. I tried to reassure him that I had plenty of things to do to get ready for school in London, or that I could go to the base to workout in the weight room or gym, but he wouldn't allow that.

Dad knew that my stepsisters had spent most of their time focusing on the men who worked out in the base gym, therefore he wouldn't have one of his daughters hanging around the base gym during the summer months. He didn't believe that I spent most of my time focusing on remaining fit. I worked out there every winter on various exercise equipment and participated in gym activities such as basketball, volleyball, indoor soccer, and floor hockey. The other fun activity was just socializing by the canteen. My favourite time at the base was learning how to safely bench press 175 pounds with my arms and 200 pounds with my legs, then spending the next hour participating in the various sports activities before going to the swimming pool and co-ed sauna. During late spring, I went swimming at the nearby community pool or the indoor pool at the base. I would also go bowling, or play recreational sports with the infantry guys in the gym.

My Dad drove me up to Ipperwash but he wasn't going to stay overnight as he and Bonnie were having marital problems and he had asked her for a divorce. Heidi and Brenda both had more work to assist with closing the cadet kitchens before we could head home to London for another winter. Most of the cadets from camp had already gone home to get ready to head back to school the following week, but my stepmother, my sisters, and I stayed behind with one of the cadet camp bus drivers. Working the kitchens in camp, my stepmother and sisters had last minute responsibilities to clear up before we could head home. As the radio reported a pending storm, most of the families cleared out before the storm was due to hit our area. With only a handful of families remaining, they were expected to be out of the campsite by 5:00 p.m. the following night. We were looking forward to leaving, as the cool winds had started to settle in and the majority of the warm summer days were already gone.

During that last night at the campsite, we sat around the campfire and listened to the radio for more details about the pending storm that was heading into our area. We learned that it was expected to hit around suppertime. Dad came back up the following evening to share a campfire with us and talk about what we planned on doing with the rest of our lives, as he made it clear that he wasn't willing to support us after high school. In fact, he wanted to make it very clear to us that we needed to have plans to move out of his home and get on with our lives, as soon as high school was completed.

While enjoying the wood burning on the campfire, Dad started to talk about the last three years, and how our lives had been estranged at times, since we had different personalities than the rest of the family and didn't quite get along. You could tell that he had something else he wanted to say when Beatrice perked up and stated that she had applied to the Canadian Forces. She was scheduled to attend her recruitment day in Cornwallis, Nova Scotia. Her twin sister Brenda was going to return to working in the kitchen of CFB London. Heidi and I figured we had another year to decide our career path, but Dad made it clear that he wanted us out of his house when we completed high school that year.

The night air was settling in, and just as we finished talking, a strong wind blew by. Brenda said, "Oh that is a cold wind coming in, I am going to bed, see you in the morning. Perhaps, if we clean up camp quick enough we can go swimming once more for the good old times before having to head home and begin living our separate lives."

The Rose
The next morning, Bonnie went off to work, and we were left to pack up the trailer while we listened to the radio. We heard that there was a warm front moving into the London, Ontario area.

Later, I was walking towards the beach with my sisters for a swim when I remembered I had to grab my towel. Standing in the trailer all by myself, I heard Bette Midler's song "The Rose" playing on the radio.

As I stood there listening to the lyrics of the song, I was frozen in thought of the years that I had passed living with my mother and now with my Cinderella stepfamily. I started crying. Deep inside, I felt like a seven-year cicada buried under the snow and wondered when I might be able to spread my wings and fly. I felt my grandmother Grace was in my presence, hugged me and gave me encouragement to move forward as I filled up with love with a gentle spiritual squeeze, realizing I was in the same trailer in which my grandma had died years earlier on June 12th, 1979.

Heidi came into the trailer just as the song was finishing and noticed me crying. She asked me what I was doing and I replied, "I feel grandmother's presence hugging me as I reflected on the song." I told her that I wondered what would happen to me when we finished living in our parent's home. Would I finally be allowed to become like the rose in the song, allowed to open up and bloom, or become too afraid to move that I wilt away until it was too late for me?

We walked back outside to meet up with our stepsisters and walked with them to the local store. Then, we headed off to the beach where we noticed some guys playing in the water among the high white caps. I started to tell my stepsisters about my hesitation to go swimming when the radio had been reporting potential tornado warnings in the area. Brenda responded, "Ah, come on, don't allow a little thing like white caps and radio announcements mess around with another potential date. Don't you remember all those beautiful days we wasted over the years because of false weather reports? Don't let some more good-looking guys get away; there might be a guy right in that water for you! Besides, you can handle the water with your years of cadets, swimming, and body building."

We walked into the water and started swimming. My stepsisters soon joined the young men, but before I could join them near the dock post where the waves weren't as big, I was caught in the white caps that kept splashing into my face. I began to swallow water and was having difficulty breathing. I realized that if I had listened to my gut feelings, and paid attention to all the warning signs, I could have prevented my current situation completely. I knew that my lack of independence, self-confidence, and ability to be easily convinced had put me into this exact situation. Although I had become very frustrated at myself I knew that I was in an emergency situation. I needed to act promptly, without wasting any precious time to reach the shore. I had already started to feel cold and tired.

In the distance, I could hear my stepsister saying, "She's a good swimmer; she is just pulling our leg. She will be fine; leave her alone." Now I was more frustrated, as this was an emergency situation. I had always been a very serious and focused person. I didn't play jokes on important matters. To those men, I was a stranger. They weren't sure if I was a joker or not, so they left me alone for a while. Soon the lifeguard in the group decided that it was a serious matter that needed to be investigated quickly.

The current swept me deeper into the water, and I swallowed more water. Bobbling up and down, I used the back kick to flutter back up towards the surface. I had my hands out to the sides, waving them in a stroking pattern. Each time I resurfaced and tried to grasp more air, I found a rolling wave of water in my face instead. When I managed to catch enough air to breathe, I tried to scream for help from the men who were swimming with my stepsisters.

Descending Depths

The water continued to splash over my head. There wasn't enough time between the waves to allow me to get enough air. I started to become disoriented each time I submerged into the water. My lungs felt as though they would explode with the pressure of so much water. I didn't have any room for air. Losing my ability to focus, I started to hyperventilate, even though the years of cadet experience and first aid classes informed me that the instant you start panicking is the moment your survival rate drops considerably.

I had run into trouble with currents and white caps before, but nothing like this. Realizing that I had taken on too much water, I was feeling cold and tired of fighting. I was not able to catch enough oxygen. I started to lose hope. I began to sink further towards the bottom, and I began to wonder if I had come to the end of my life right there, only 100 meters away from my family. I was terrified, as I tried desperately to survive or have somebody notice that I was in a serious situation.

That is when I took another breath of air. I accepted my fate and began feeling that my emotional, mental, and spiritual bodies were ready to release everything to God. "Is this my destiny?" Then, I began to rapidly pray, "My Lord, God, and Saviour please, be gentle on those I leave behind. Tell them that I love them and that I am glad they have been in my life, especially my twin." I reflected quickly on all the things we had gone through together, sharing special moments, and songs.

I was reaching the surface! I could see the sky! I was getting hopeful, but then another huge wave came and struck me down.

It then became more difficult and stressful. My patience and hope of survival were running out with all the water in my lungs. The moment came when my body felt extremely heavy. I started losing consciousness and control of my bodily functions as I involuntarily began urinating and vomiting each time the wave brought me to the surface. I knew that the window of opportunity for survival had greatly diminished. I resurfaced one last time. I tried to yell for help, but had no strength left. Stretching my right hand as far as I could straight up towards the sky, gave me one last glimmer of hope that one of those guys who were with my stepsisters might have pulled away from the pack to help me. I hadn't noticed if anybody had paid much attention to my situation. I had been too busy trying to stay afloat over the last ten minutes, since my crisis began.

Still sinking, I kept my right hand stretched up in the direction of the surface to try and give anyone who might have tried to save me a chance to have me resurface from the water. I didn't want to believe that my life was over. My life up to this point had been full of painful experiences, a loveless family, and an incredible amount of suffering. There were a few members of my family that I knew would occasionally think of me. Their lives would go unchanged whether I lived or died. So, I prayed that they would find happiness wherever their futures took them. The bond between my twin sister and me was different, so I prayed that she would be okay.

I continued to sink to the bottom of the lake. I started to fade into unconsciousness. I began to fade into the endless deep sleep of death. Up to this point, I had been so scared to enter into this realm. Now I closed my eyes. I found peace the moment that I had come to accept my own demise. The brightest of all lights appeared, totally surrounding me in the most beautiful tender love. Shockingly, I began to receive the deep-seated love that I had been looking for all of my life. It was just on the other side of life. I would actually find love. Gratefully, I embraced my new path and all the love it gave me.

My physical body no longer mattered. I was going into my spiritual body. I became more aware of my spiritual presence. All the other spirits within this lake came to greet me. In the distance, I could see a spirit ship. I was given information about its size, age, what it looked like, what it was made of, how it sank, and the approximate year it had sunk. The ship had suffered a large hole in the port bow and sank within minutes, taking the lives of at least 33 passengers and crewmen. The vessel, built in 1863, was a 200-foot twin-screw wooden passenger and freight steamer, and it had sunk in less than five minutes.

I felt the presence of many other spirits in the water; about two hundred spirits in total surrounded me, and were approaching me. They gracefully welcomed me. There was a man who seemed to be leading the rest of the spirits towards me. He told another to get behind him. They were to approach me gently and not scare me. An additional one hundred other spirits in the water came from all different directions to greet me. I felt as though I had stumbled upon a spiritual realm of unrested gentle souls. I felt completely comfortable with what was happening to me spiritually. I no longer felt that we were in water. Rather, I felt like we were in a different, mystical, floating dimension, where time stood still.

Moments later, I felt a physical person from the surface of the water touch the tip of my right hand. All the spirits disappeared, as my spiritual body became stuck going back into my physical body. It was like a genie in a bottle. Spiritually, I was completely between two different worlds. I was neither totally present in the spiritual world nor in the physical realm. I was halfway between both worlds, at a crossroads between two alternative dimensions, drifting in a state of limbo. My spiritual-self waited for my physical-self to decide in which of the two realms it would remain.

When my spiritual body returned to my physical form, I started to become more aware of my own presence. The physical person above me pulled me towards the surface of the lake. They dragged me along behind. I reached the surface of the water. I came back into my physical self and heard two people talking. It was a woman and a man. The woman asked the man, "Did you get her?" He replied, "Yes, I have her. Help me get her to the shore." As they started to drag me on to shore, I started to become more conscious of my physical surroundings. I felt the surface of the water on my face and the sun beaming down on me. He was keeping me aware of my present situation. As I started to get some air into my lungs, I was thankful for being saved, and for what I had just seen in the spiritual realm moments earlier.

All the time they were bringing me to the shore, both of them remained calm, which assisted me in feeling more comfortable and relaxed about my current situation. When they got me to the beach, my legs were dragging behind the rest of my body. I was lethargic and exhausted from the whole ordeal. They laid me on my back as the man over top of me pushed on my lungs, administered CPR, and rolled me onto to my right side, repeating this procedure several times until all the water that had entered my lungs was gone. He turned me on my side and put me into a cradle position, left knee bent in the recovery position. He then told my twin to keep an eye on me, and took our towels and covered me with them. He then proceeded back to the docks with my stepsister Brenda. I lay on the beach beside my twin sister who provided me support as I recovered.

At about 6:00 p.m., I had gained enough strength to start walking with my sisters back to the trailer. The wind had picked up enough sand that we had to cover most of our faces in order to avoid getting the flying sand particles into our eyes. The strength of the wind made it hard to catch our breath. We heard thunderstorms and saw bolts of lightning all around us.

We stopped in one of our friend's trailers located close to the beach after walking a half an hour. We paused temporarily to catch our breath before heading back on the path to our own trailer.

Windy Night

When we got back to our trailer, our stepmother decided that the weather was too bad to drive home. We were invited to spend some time during the evening playing cards inside, but at bedtime Bonnie ordered Heidi and me to go out and sleep in the tent-trailer as our own grandmother's hard-top trailer was just for our dad who was staying in London, herself our stepmother and her daughters. Heidi and I begged her to allow us to sleep in the spare beds as the tornado seemed to be right outside of our door, but she was firmly against it and reminded us that we were not her daughters and therefore, it was out of the question.

We returned to the tent-trailer just in time. The strong winds in the area and the bangs and crashes seemed like the storm was hitting us hard. We stayed curled up in our beds, as we had done in our youth. We were hoping that whatever was on the outside of our door would soon go away.

We felt what seemed to be the tent-trailer lifting off the ground and dropping a couple of feet towards the tree line. It was causing damage to the tarp that we were inside of. That night, lying in my cot in the tent-trailer getting wet as the storm had passed, I thought about how close I had come to dying, and how lucky I was to have survived. I wondered about all the lives that had been lost on the ghost ship and surrounding liners. I wondered how they must have felt when they took their last breaths, and who greeted them when it was their turn to die.

By morning, when we came out, we noticed that the tent-trailer had actually moved two feet into the tree line. The winds could no longer move us as the low flying branches near our trailer had pinned down the tarp. We were both thankful for another day despite the scares that night. Heidi and I hugged, as we were grateful that we had managed to get through the tornado together, and swore that no matter where we went in life we would always be there for each other.

We left camp early that morning, and on our drive home Bonnie turned on the radio and we listened to the weather forecast. We heard about all the places that had been affected by the tornado. This time, Ipperwash and Grand Bend hadn't been spared. In fact, we had been in the water when the beginning of the cycle started to come inland and some of the hardtop trailers had suffered severe damage.

The radio announced a damaging tornado had touched down just southwest of London. It proceeded to rip through the White Oaks subdivision and damaged approximately 600 homes, causing harm to 30 people as a result. Over the northern portion of the city, torrential downpours dropped 40-60 mm of rain in about an hour, and were accompanied by gusty winds. There was one last brief touchdown near Bothell, northeast of Thamesville, Kent County shortly after the London tornado lifted.

4

FLATLINE CHILDBIRTH

Death, taxes and childbirth! There's never any convenient time for any of them.

—Margaret Mitchell, *Gone With the Wind*

Bundles of Joy

By 1987, when I was 20 years old, I had married my first husband, Robert. We were adjusting to married life and the eventual arrival of our first baby. By the time I was eight months pregnant, my mother was diagnosed with stage-four cancer. She was in her last stages of life. My marriage was experiencing challenges with financial constraints causing us tremendous stress. Shortly after giving birth to our daughter Stephine, I was discharged from the Peterborough General Hospital, and went down to the greyhound station to book a drive to London to stay with my twin sister for a couple of weeks in order to have visits with our mother, who was residing with our brother.

While I visited my mother at her bedside, she stated, "I am sorry that I wasn't a better mother for you during your childhood, but I will always be there in spirit for your children, my grandchildren." I didn't believe her since I didn't believe anyone had control over where we go after we die. But she seemed to think we did, and I wasn't prepared to argue with her either; as a result, her words were heard but not believed.

While I was away, my husband Robert received a promotion from the local shoe department store where he had been working as a sales representative. He became an Assistant Manager at the Upper Canada Mall in Newmarket. Robert requested that I come home immediately in order to assist him in preparing our family's belongings for our move at the end of the month.

We established our footing in the Newmarket area by finding our residence, the specific store, and a family doctor. We had just moved into a motel near Robert's work when I received a phone call from Heidi to return back to London, as my mom's doctor noted that her breathing had changed and that she didn't have long to live. But with limited means and a young family, we didn't have any emergency funds for me to travel back to London. So I sent my blessings. A few weeks later, on March 31st, 1988, she passed. She was only a few weeks away from her next birthday and our wedding anniversary.

I called up my Dad to inform him that mom had recently died and that I wondered how I could get to London for her funeral. Dad volunteered to drive me there and back for a fraction of the cost of gasoline.

A Second Child

The following month, when Stephine was seven months old, I was told we were expecting our second child. I was surprised to be pregnant right away. I spent most of my time raising Stephine and keeping myself busy with activities for the two of us, and gynecologist appointments.

Robert and I had different RH factors, which directly increased health concerns during pregnancies. There was a possibility of the fetus inheriting Robert's blood type, which would have increased the chances of my blood system reacting against our unborn fetus as a foreign intruder. We were cautious about this with Stephine, but my pregnancy with her was safe. That was not the case with our second child. We found out early on in my second pregnancy that the fetus did, in fact, have Robert's blood type, therefore my blood's antibodies started to attack our unborn child as she continued to grow.

I was continually having Braxton Hicks contractions, causing our baby's system to become increasingly defensive against my own blood system. An amniocentesis was ordered to monitor our baby's blood and to examine its overall health. An ultrasound was performed to examine the condition of the placenta to ensure that it would remain intact. The tests detected no abnormalities, even though the heart rate of our baby had dropped temporarily.

After the examination, I lay in the hospital bed for what seemed like an eternity. However, the moment I got up to leave, I started having contractions, which forced me to be admitted to hospital, and an IV was administered. After twenty-four hours, the hospital released me when my health returned to the expected conditions for a woman in her second trimester. Upon my release from the hospital, I was given orders for increased bed rest, and decreased magnesium sulphate, which was believed to assist in decreasing the risk of my physical conditions. Through this process, my neighbour looked after our oldest daughter Stephine, whenever I had any immediate medical concerns. However, my hospital stays continued to lengthen and arrangements had to be made for our older daughter to stay with our family.

The blood types were colliding, causing several false contractions, which required spending weeks in the hospital. My most notable visit was on November 11th, when my gynecologist at the hospital had repeatedly been administering tocolytics (anti-contraction medication, or labour suppressants) in order to suppress what he thought to be my premature labour. By suppressing my contractions over several days in the hospital, they were able to prolong my child's arrival. I didn't know if my baby was still alive, as he kept ordering the nurses to continue with this treatment.

Labour Pains

Eventually, I went back into labour the evening of December 8, 1988. I was scared that my doctor would stop the labour process again; as a result I refused to leave the house until I knew for sure he couldn't stop me from delivery. Hours later into the early morning hours, I gingerly walked from our master bedroom to the living room to allow my husband Robert to get more sleep. I had lain on the couch through contractions for the next several hours in increased pain, until I couldn't help but start pushing. My husband was asleep down the corridor in our bedroom, and I yelled for his assistance to get me to the hospital.

By the time I managed to get him awake and into the living room, I had already started pushing heavily. It was 4:25 am. We didn't have a phone, a car, or a neighbour that my husband felt comfortable about waking up in the middle of the night. So, he needed to run down to the corner store or to our local Tim Horton's to call an ambulance. Before he took off running down the road, he told me that our daughter was sleeping in her crib and to try and keep the noise down so as to not wake her.

Luckily, when he got to the nearest plaza there was a taxicab waiting to see if there were any calls coming in from the local pubs. My husband approached it and asked him if he would take me to the hospital. When Robert got back to the apartment, I walked up the thirteen steps to get outside where the cab driver was waiting for me. Robert said that he would be by in a little while, as he remained at home to watch our eldest daughter Stephine. I suggested he have one of our neighbours watch her, but Robert insisted that it would be unfair to wake them despite having made previous arrangements with them. He said that he was going back to bed and would report to the hospital in the morning.

The cab driver drove me to the hospital. While I looked for the money Robert had given me, he rushed inside and fetched me a wheel chair. I paid him upon his return. He wheeled me into the doors of the hospital, and then left as he received another call.

Upon entering the hospital, I asked for assistance to register me quickly, but the receptionist's response was, "You have to wait for your turn, and should be quiet." I angrily said, "Sure!" as I continued to push and the baby's head started to crown. "Sure, I will just wait here and be quiet, while I give birth!"

She said, "What did you say?"

I said, "I will try to be quiet, while I give birth!"

She paused in shock, and said, "I will get you a person to take you upstairs, right away."

She immediately requested the patient she was currently seeing to please give her a minute while she called upstairs and she picked up her phone at her desk. Within minutes, an orderly arrived in the emergency room, introduced himself to me and asked if I could hold my belongings so that he could take me upstairs to the Labour and Delivery room.

Flatline Childbirth

Within the first 15 minutes after arriving at the hospital, I was on an operating room table, with the doctor telling me to stop pushing as the cord was around my baby's throat, cutting off my baby's blood supply. While I was pushing, the pressure inadvertently travelled to my heart and stopped it.

Suddenly, I felt a sense of total peace and tranquility. The people, place and situation that my physical body was presently experiencing were no longer a worry of mine. Instead, I felt my spirit separate from my body, and any care or worry I had were gone.

I felt totally stress-free as a vibrating, pure, white light surrounded me. I began to feel completely at peace in an ultimate, encompassing love. I was no longer in the room in which my physical presence was experiencing stress. Instead, my spiritual presence floated into a space filled with white light so bright that all I could sense was my mother, and her voice repeatedly yelling at me: "Go back! Go back!"

Curious where this voice I heard all around me was coming from, my spiritual presence pressed forward to the bright, vibrating, white light. I sensed a pulling feeling from my physical presence lying on the operating table, as though it was trying to pull my spiritual presence back to it. However, I kept pressing forwards, as I had a higher sense and desire to see what was becoming clearer to me in the mist of the white light.

The voice increased its eagerness to force me to "Go Back! Go Back!" However, I tried not to notice the pressuring concern that this spirit seemed to have, wanting me to return to my physical body.

I was fighting my physical body's encompassing strings attached to every morsel of my spiritual presence. It felt like my spiritual presence was trapped and being pulled by elastics attached to every cell of my body. My physical presence was pulling me back with a thud while my spiritual presence pressed forward, closer to the light.

I did not realize at the time that this threshold, created by the tremendous pull of my spiritual and physical presence on each other, was actually the threshold between life and death. The medical staff worked on my physical body, fighting desperately to keep my body alive. They engaged the defibrillator, as my spiritual presence fought to go back to the light and the sound of my mother's voice. Travelling back to where my spirit had already travelled before, I noticed an outline of a city wall that had mist surrounding it. I pressed forward towards my mother's voice, anxious to see her. Her voice became abrupt. "Go Back! Go back! It's not your time."

Having just spiritually travelled down a long corridor towards a white light, I could see and feel the presence of my spiritual family members coming towards me, to greet me. As I came closer, it looked like I was approaching a gate, but soon I could make out that it was people who came to greet me. Their heads were the tops of the picket fence, their shoulders decorative triads, and their joined hands made the fence look complete.

The spirits who greeted me, I recognized as my mother, grandparents and uncles, some of whom I had never met in the physical form and only heard about. All seemed to have a spiritual connection with me, as they were linked together to greet me. As I got closer to the light, the people seemed to separate in the middle to allow me to travel past them. The tunnel seemed dark again until mom re-appeared in front of me.

As I continued to press forward, I spotted her. This time she was sitting on what looked like a large round water fountain with a large two feet high cement cylinder surface around it. It seemed very peaceful and beautiful. The colours were vibrant and bright, almost blinding. Mom seemed to be speaking to somebody else. Although I couldn't make out the figure, I could hear the voice of the other person. Mom peacefully and slowly approached me and told me, "Go back, it's not your time. You have to go back. You have things you have to do. You must go back!"

I asked, "How will I know what I am supposed to do?"

"It will come to you in dreams, messages, and in your own feelings. Follow them all, especially your feelings. That is why you have them. When it is your time, we will all be here to greet you. You will finally be welcome to stay, but not until then."

Suddenly, it seemed as though I had passed a thin veil. Things waiting for me on the other side began to reveal themselves. I felt and saw a quiet populated area where many spirits seemed to have their own assignments and schedules. The area had gardens, buildings, a library and vast land which to me seemed very familiar, and was what I presumed Israel would look like. The buildings were lightly coloured, clay like, with different sized structures, but nothing that seemed to be more than several floors high; no sky scrapers.

In the distance I could see a mountain. The Holy Mountain intrigued me to press forward. As I came closer to it, I noticed seven rows of angels. Behind these angels was Jesus, wearing his long white gown, with a brown open robe draped over his shoulders. As I approached, he rose up to greet me, but all of a sudden, before he could speak to me, I returned to physical presence with a thud, as though I had just fallen from a great height back into my physical body. I spotted the nurse coming towards me, rubbing the two defibrillator pads roughly while she was under tremendous tension and in a panic.

I asked her, "What are you doing?"

"You already flat-lined twice, and it looks like you're going again. I want to make sure that you don't, especially since I really had to fight to bring you back the second time."

I responded in shock, "Please, do me a favour …"

"Sure, anything!"

"Please, count how many doctors and nurses are in the room."

"Sure, why?"

"Just do it!"

She counted and recounted, "7."

"Then you can put the paddles away, I am not going to go again."

"How do you know?"

"I just do, as my number is 7. I'm safe; I'm not going again, but thanks for not giving up on me."

NICU

Hearing my baby crying for the first time made me catch my bearings on where I actually was. I asked about the baby. The nurse responded, "You have a beautiful baby girl, but she was having problems. The cord was around her throat, and she had lost a lot of oxygen. The triage nurse will have to rush her down to the NICU (Neonatal Intensive Care Unit) as soon as the doctors are finished with her here. What is the NICU? It is for infants that are born with severe complications and are having problems breathing. We need to have her checked out by their staff to make sure that she is going to be all right. When she has received a clean bill of health, you can see her."

"But, I want to see my baby now, please."

"I am sorry, but there is no time for that; time is too precious at this moment."

"Please, just for a second. Can I hold her for a second just to give her a kiss, just in case she doesn't make it through?"

She checked with the doctors and responded, "Okay, just for a second, as every second counts in moments like this. Only a second, that is it!"

The pediatric doctor and two assistant nurses were rushing around, and the room seemed hyperactive and stressed. I gave my daughter a kiss, and then she was rushed down the hall to the NICU. As I lay on the operating table, I could hear them running her down the hallway. Then the sound disappeared when they opened the heavy doors and went further down the hallway. I wondered if I would ever see or hear my baby alive again.

Over the next couple of days, the nursing staff watched over both of us carefully. For the first five days, Jaccinta-Marie wasn't allowed to come out of her NICU unit. She was in a severe medical condition and required secure room isolation in order to gain enough antibodies to protect her from any airborne pathogens. The doctors wouldn't release her from the NICU until she was able to handle any natural airborne diseases, as her immune system was very weak. The doctors weren't sure if her body had the strength she needed to be able to protect her.

I felt empty inside, and wondered what I could have done differently in order to prevent such things from happening to my baby. I felt so lonely for my children, and hoped that Jaccinta-Marie would be able to go home soon.

A few days later the doctor explained to me that both of us had stopped breathing during the birth process and had to be revived. She was also born dry and scaly. Their explanation was that all the IVs to assist with stopping the baby's birth had been incorrect, that the doctor had made a mistake in his calculations, and that she should have been born as per the last set of major contractions on November 11th and not on December 9th, when she was born.

My baby had been in my womb an additional month, and therefore had no amniotic fluid to keep her moist. That is why she had the cord wrapped around her throat at birth. There wasn't any room around her for the cord to float, and the sack was completely empty. They were surprised that she wasn't stillborn due to the lack of liquid in the placenta.

It was a miracle that she had survived at all, but now that she had, it was critically evident that she required a lot of support during the initial forty-eight hours of the five days she was in the NICU.

Those forty-eight hours went by easier than expected with the help and guidance of the Holy Spirit and the team of doctors and nurses in the York County Hospital. After five days, all systems were in place for her to be moved from the NICU to my room. Within another twenty-four hours she was discharged to go home with me.

Upon her discharge, my gynecologist came into my room, double checking to make sure that nobody was around to hear him. He stated, "I'm sorry you had such difficulty with your birth. I'm glad that your baby and you are okay. I just wanted to give you an apology for stopping all your last labour contractions. I went back over my notes. It seems that I made a few miscalculations; you should have given birth last month. Despite all the possibility of complications, you and your baby have been discharged from the hospital today. Your baby seems to be very good except that she is being discharged with an easily dislocating left hip. She will be required to wear three pairs of diapers for the next six months while she gains more stability in that leg. In time, watch for signs of more medical complications such as a slanted spine, a medical condition called scoliosis."

Back Home

The baby and her new big sister, Stephine, were adjusting to sharing their parents. The next medical appointment at our family's doctor showed us that everything was adjusting on schedule.

However, after one of our outpatient appointments with our family doctor, my husband and I stopped with our children to get a small bite to eat at a local restaurant. The sandwich we got seemed to taste a little strange, but we were all extremely hungry and didn't have a lot of money, so we ate it and walked home. However, the next several hours proved horrible, as we all started to vomit and have diarrhea.

That night, my mother's spirit seemed to come through the top far corner of our bedroom while my husband and I were taking turns running to the bathroom to empty our stomachs. That terrified me. I had seen spirits all of my life, but this time it was only her face in the top far corner. Although it originally came to me as one foot in length, it instantly grew to over five feet as though to scare me to know that she meant business. Upon my husband's return from the bathroom I informed him what had just transpired. He said, "Then I guess we better listen as she is trying to tell us something." When we arrived at the hospital, we were all diagnosed with severe food poisoning. We were lucky that three out of four of us had not died. It was reported that the restaurant we had eaten in was under investigation and was immediately shut down due to inconsumable food products.

Mom's Warning

Once we were discharged from the hospital, we again returned to our routine lives. Robert went back to work while I remained at home taking care of our young children. In fact, Robert received a new **promotion to Manager** and we were scheduled to move to Ottawa to open the new store at Billings Bridge Mall. We were looking forward to the move and needed to prepare as everything was going to take some time before we resettled again. In order to prepare, I booked Jaccinta-Marie for her first needle before she was supposed to get it. Instead of having it at eight weeks, she would have it at five weeks old.

I made the appointment and she had her needle. Everything seemed to be fine. Although she was a little groggy and grumpy, all went smoothly. The girls and I left the doctor's office and went home, and I put the girls to bed; Stephine into her crib, and Jaccinta-Marie eventually settled down on my bed with pillows around her for extra protection so she wouldn't slide off as she continued to sleep.

To my surprise, I was startled when I heard my mother's voice yelling at me repetitively: "Go get the baby!" I didn't understand what the issue was or why I would think that I heard her voice. Although I had become accustomed to hearing and seeing spirits, I wasn't comfortable knowing that I was different than most people in regards to the spirit realm. I quickly turned on the hall light at one end of my long hallway leading up to my master bedroom, and in the doorway of my dark room stood my mother's figure. She was standing directly in my doorway and although I quickly walked over to her and asked her to move, she remained in the same spot, as my mother's spirit was blocking me from entering my bedroom to go check on my daughter.

I yelled again, but she just wouldn't move, so I proceeded to walk through her spirit. I had a terrible warping feeling, as though I was stretching the fibres of my mother's spirit. In reality, it lasted for a few seconds, but the sensation felt like it took a few minutes. Now, I knew exactly what it felt like to have bent space and time. I felt incredibly weird for having just walked through my mother's spirit. Trying to recapture my thoughts, I stood about four feet away from my doorway by the time I had surpassed our intertwined spiritual entanglement and been able to get my bearings.

I walked over to my baby lying in my bed, and instantly ran with her out of my bedroom down the long corridor and into some light. When I noticed that my baby's face had turned blue, I immediately started CPR, hitting her between her shoulders with the heel of my hand to get her to breathe, then turning her over quickly to breath in both her nose and mouth. After about a few minutes, that seemed like eternity, of doing this with my newborn's life hanging on by a string, she started to breathe again on her own. I breathed a sigh of relief and ran to the next-door neighbour's, requested them to take care of Stephine who was still sleeping in her crib, and asked if the husband could please take us to the hospital.

Jaccinta-Marie

Jaccinta-Marie was admitted right away and went through a battery of tests that all proved negative. The doctor asked us if anyone new had been around me, visitors, relatives, friends or children since the last time we had been in hospital; anybody with a cough or cold even while you were pregnant, anything unusual.

Both my husband and I were puzzled as to whom we had come in contact with. We normally stayed to ourselves, and our closest family members were over three hours away. I then recalled that one day after one of my last gynecologist appointments, upon arriving home, I found my landlord walking around inside of our apartment coughing. She had just recently returned from a trip overseas and had come back with what she called the whooping cough.

The doctor replied, "That's it, when she came into your home, she contaminated your residence, which affected your unborn fetus. When she was born and given the vaccination for the same thing, it affected her breathing. Luckily, with your previous military background and first aid training, you were able to handle the emergency when it occurred, or she might not be here today."

The doctor said there wasn't anything I could do now except to make sure that we take care of Jaccinta-Marie, and advised we keep her in the hospital for a week under observation. During that time, Jaccinta-Marie went through a number of tests including one that had stopped her from breathing again. By the end of the following week, her temperature had risen to 109°, requiring an emergency blood transfusion. Luckily, by the end of the second week, she was discharged with a loaner heart monitor.

We then moved to our next location, Ottawa. Jaccinta-Marie had recovered, but by six months old, she was diagnosed with scoliosis. By the time she was 27 months old, she had to have back surgery to insert a Harrington Rod.

5

PHOENIX TRIP

Jesus, take the wheel. Take it from my hands 'cause I can't do this on my own!

—Carrie Underwood, *Jesus, Take the Wheel*

The Promotion

Robert was excited about his latest promotion in Ottawa, as a store manager. He was only twenty-two years old and was under a tremendous amount of pressure. However, he felt he could handle all of his new responsibilities: staffing, maintaining proper layout, promotions, and keeping sales within the expected range for this quality of store, as well as being a father of two and maintaining our small family.

However, by the winter of 1989, I was 22 years old, and my young family consisted of four members living in a one-bedroom apartment. We were barely making ends meet on one income of less than $25,000 a year. We were classified as the working poor. We were constantly struggling with each other, having matrimonial issues, as our finances were gradually getting worse with our growing family. We were searching for new ways to reduce spending and make our money last until the end of the month. With two young children at home, we were forced to look for alternative methods to solve this growing deficiency.

We knew that I needed to find a cashier position working in either the evening or nights to offset some of our financial shortage. While Robert continued to work during the day, I took care of the kids, and in the evening, we would trade-off the responsibility of the kids; while I go to work, he would took care of our children. Within a month, I had found a full-time midnight shift at our local convenience store.

Sharing the responsibility of childcare eliminated the need for a babysitter or sending the girls to nursery school, which would have depleted my earnings. I contacted the Ontario Secondary School Board to obtain a copy of my high school diploma in the hope of finding a better job, but I discovered that I didn't actually graduate, and was lacking my grade twelve English class. I had skipped the end of grade 12 to start my training with the 22nd Service Battalion. I was told that all my classes were in good standing and I would still graduate, but that wasn't the case. As a result, in September I began filling two evenings a week attending night school for that credit, between taking care of the kids and working my midnight position.

However, somebody contacted the CAS office and requested on my behalf for additional help in a respite program for a few hours a week, to allow me to get caught up on sleep and do errands. As I was taking care of the kids during the day, attending school in the evenings and working as a cashier over the midnight hours, little time was left to do anything else, including sleep.

However, on February 9, 1990, Robert was fired from his full-time job at the shoe store and with two children and a third on the way, we could no longer afford to remain in Ottawa. Luckily, I had just completed my English credit. We were preparing to move into his mother's upper attic, bachelor apartment in Peterborough, Ontario, but first wanted to take our long overdue honeymoon, which we were able to do with his severance package. We hoped it would strengthen our already crumbling marriage. We had arranged to stay at his mother's and sleep on her living room floor upon our return from our trip, until we qualified for a government accommodation.

We sent money to his mother for our projected expenses before taking our trip. We decided to go to the annual camping event being held in Phoenix by the Society for Creative Anachronism (SCA), an international historical group we were involved with that recreated Medieval European cultures. One of our good friends in the SCA, Jeff, who was attending the event decided to come with us to help share the travel expenses.

Last minute, Heidi decided to babysit for us for the full ten daysof our honeymoon, which was a blessing, as it meant that we would not have to stop every forty minutes to attend to the demands of screaming kids. Once we left London, we took a two-and-a-half day trip with nothing planned, and no detouring delays. Heidi begged us not to take the trip as she had a strong premonition that we were going to get into a car accident. I reconfirmed with her whether she was comfortable with taking care of our girls. She said that she was fine and not to worry; she reminded me to take extra caution while driving.

Phoenix Trip

After dropping off the girls, we drove for an additional two hours without stopping. Because we shared the driving, we made up for the time we had lost making the girls comfortable in their car seats, arriving on the Detroit-Canadian border at 12:30 a.m. The two border guards asked us to unload our entire car's baggage, as they made us go through every inch of our camping equipment, food, clothing and everything else we had. They had us throw out all food products and toiletries including our toothpaste, and by the time we put everything that we were allowed to keep back into the vehicle, we were miserable and tired, losing all the time we had just made up. We crossed the border about 2 a.m. We were exhausted but drove another two hours before calling it a night and pulling into a family-run motel.

We rented two separate rooms for a few hours of sleep for the first full-night sleep we had since we left Ottawa a day-and-a-half earlier. Feeling rejuvenated after about six hours of sleep, we started off again on our journey. We set off for a long-haul drive, initially through areas of Elvis Presley monuments as we travelled towards our destination. We went through Louisville, KY, and Nashville, TN, before viewing the gates of Graceland in Memphis. We then went through Arkansas, past Oklahoma and Amarillo, TX, before going through part of the Salt River Canyon in New Mexico. By taking a tourist approach to our driving, we were turning a delayed honeymoon into a real adventure. It also allowed us to see several parts of the Grand Canyon and valleys surrounding the various areas, which we might have otherwise missed by going straight through to Phoenix.

By the time we stopped in another motel, we had already been driving for nineteen hours. We spotted a 'Circle K' gas bar and restaurant. It was located 10 km northeast of Tonto National Forest. We stopped to fill the tank with gasoline, as well as our two extra jerry cans in our trunk in case of emergencies. We grabbed a bite to eat and switched drivers.

I had asked the cashier, "How much longer before we reach Phoenix, AZ?" She said, "It's just past the canyon, straight ahead down that road, but heed my warnings: Do not try and travel that canyon highway through the night. It is an assured deathtrap; there are steep inclines, sharp turns with dangerous angles, and no warnings, flags, or markers of any kind. Have you ever stopped at the Apache National Forest?" We answered yes. "Then, you better not try the road ahead of you. It's ten times worse. Even the locals won't travel through the canyon until daylight, when they are fully awake and alert. It is very dangerous; that is why there are so many motels for travelers to stop for the night. You guys are smart to ask these questions, as it might have just saved your lives. Those who do not heed all these road signs or warnings by reading the large boards on the side of the highway, or stop and speak to the locals from the area, tend not to make it through the night. Many have tried and failed."

She then said many foreigners do not ask these questions. They continue to drive, costing them their lives only to have their loved ones reporting them missing a few days later.

As we travelled 5 km down the road to a motel before the canyon, we couldn't help but notice multiple road signs warning of steep declines and dangerous roads within the canyon. We decided to listen to the cashier and the locals who had come into the gas bar while we were speaking to her. We slept in the motel on the highway and started off again first thing the next morning.

Grand Canyon

We woke up early, got into the car after breakfast and proceeded towards the canyon. Within the first five minutes, we were travelling down a twenty-five degree hill, facing straight into a ravine that held thousands of feet of open space, waiting to swallow us whole. Driving closer to the edge of the ravine, we felt a very sharp curve, like we were sliding into the side of the cliff with the weight of our heavy camping equipment forcing us down further and faster than my husband could control the station wagon.

It was as though we were travelling down a rocky roller coaster with no tracks. If we were to miss a single planned step, we would go over the cliff and land in the bottom of the ravine, which I could see clearly from my vantage point in the passenger seat, which terrified me. The road at the end of the steep incline was so narrow that there was no room to put roadside barriers on these cliffs. Without any markings along the steep and tangled road, we had to rely solely on my husband's ability to drive slowly through this dangerous terrain and we immediately understood how others could drive right off the cliffs.

All I could do was encourage my husband in his driving, and hang on tightly with my nails digging into the dashboard of our station wagon. We were glad that we had lost some extra weight at the border. By the time we were finished the two-hour drive, I had imprinted my fingernails into the dashboard—sure evidence of the intensity of our trip through the mountain cliffs.

That year, the Estrella War—the camping event held by the SCA—was held near the Estrella Mountain Regional Park, just west of Phoenix, AZ. The event was February 17th-19th, but it was extremely warm. Being pregnant, I volunteered as a water girl, as it provided me the best opportunity to remain close to water while in the desert. As part of the event activities, the men reenacted a massive medieval war, dressed in traditional knight garb, and mock-fighting each other in various events, such as jousting and sword fighting. I stayed close to my husband in case any emergencies arose due to the heat of the day.

The next day, when camp concluded, we decided to travel a different, safer route, rather than the dangerous one we had travelled to get to Phoenix. We travelled north to Flagstaff, AZ, then straight east through Albuquerque, NM. It was reported to be a much safer highway with markings and paved shoulders on the side of the road and easier curves and inclines. We decided to spend the morning exploring Phoenix, prior to purchasing some groceries for the long trip back home.

When we changed direction, the elevation changed and so did the weather as we turned from the I-17 to I-40. The heat of the desert was instantly replaced with a deep cold winter night. The weather changed so rapidly with a freak snowstorm and it got so cold that it reminded us of exactly what we had left behind in Ottawa, several months of "Old Canadian Winter." Now, with the weather change, the road conditions became unpredictable. We were driving into weather made for Canadian winters. This became a bittersweet moment for us, having just left this type of weather back home. After experiencing the warmth of the desert and a great camping weekend that had been loaded full of fun activities, we were overtired and suffering from heat exhaustion. As we drove northeast towards Canada and hit the winter winds, it reminded me of my kids and I began to miss them incredibly.

By the time we got between Laguna and Albuquerque, NM, the weather had changed so much we wanted to turn around and stay for another couple of months, but we had to get home for our kids. As such, we had to 'keep moving forward.' At 10:00 p.m., we couldn't see two feet in front of us. Travelling down to the base of the Mesita Mountain near Marmon Cavern made it seem like we were definitely driving in what seemed to be another Canadian winter storm.

After travelling all day, we listened as the radio announced that the area was experiencing a freak winter storm that they haven't had in a decade. I had started driving about an hour earlier and being Canadian, I felt rather comfortable, and probably cocky. I had driven through various winter storms in the past, so I didn't pay close enough attention to the weather warnings. This storm contained a high 37 mph gust of wind and sustained a 20 mph wind speed with a snow depth of two inches; and in the late hour, a fresh 1.2 inches of snow had dropped the temperature to 10° F (minus 12° C).

My driving speed reduced from 100 to 60 km/hr. or lower, depending on the conditions of the road travelling down I-40 around the Continental Divide. I felt rather comfortable about my driving, as I had been trained by the military to drive many of their vehicles, such as jeeps, trucks and heavy duty two-and-a-half tonne trucks, carrying twelve men in the back. I had even driven other vehicles transporting both officers and enlisted men from one base to another, or from London to the Toronto Airport.

I also had experience driving more difficult terrains, and driving using night goggles. The visibility and quietness were weirdly similar, and reminded me of those days. But this experience was quite different, as I was driving with two men sleeping in the car. Jeff was beside me in the passenger seat, and Robert was behind me, sprawled out on the back seat. I was trying to be quiet to let them sleep, but the wind blowing across our vehicle was deafening. The high gusts of wind pushed the car across the road, making it more difficult to maneuver.

We were alone in the dark, during an unexpected snowstorm in the middle of a desert. The winds had steadily grown stronger for the past half-hour since we started the gentle climb to the top of the mountain. The roads seemed to be getting more slippery. Each gust of wind under our station wagon was pushing us, from side to side and front to back; depending on which angle the car was facing into the wind. Reaching the top of the mountain, we realized just how much the landscape had been covered with snow a couple of inches deep over the desert. It was a very unusual sight for the residents of the area.

The condition of the roadway was one they were not used to travelling. As a result, most of them got off and stayed in their homes. Yet for us Canadians, it was a harsh reminder of exactly what was awaiting for us for several more months back home.

Reaching the other side of the mountain, I noticed again just how barren the highway was. Our car was the only vehicle on the road for miles around, except for an eighteen-wheel transport truck that was coming towards us down another hill that we would eventually have to climb after our descent into the valley.

The Descent

Noticing how barren the highway really was heightened my awareness of the appalling highway conditions and just how potentially dangerous they were. Unfortunately for us, we lacked the funds to stay in the motels that we passed a few miles behind us. The little bit of money we had left was needed for our food and gasoline expenses. We needed to stretch our funds as far as possible.

Starting the descent, I noticed several places on the highway that had patches of black ice, which I tried to avoid by using both sides of the road. It would have prevented any additional traffic behind me to pass, but I continued since I had not seen anybody for hours. I felt rather confident that we weren't going to either. I figured, I didn't have to worry about traffic reaching me before I got to the bottom of the hill. I started my descent down the mountain slowly, reassured that my years of driving had paid off and that we were going to be safe.

I felt pretty confident that we were going to make it safely until I noticed a large sheet of black ice that stretched across the entire width of the highway, leaving no dry patch that I could drive on. As I hit the ice, my body became immediately overwhelmed with fear, and I slammed my foot on the brake as the car was still descending the mountain against the force of the brakes. Braking had lifted the back end of the station wagon up into the air as the front end lowered. As the car started to flip, I could see the concrete coming towards our front window. I couldn't believe the fear that my whole body instantly felt. I had lost total control of the vehicle, and we were going to smash against the road, face first, and there was not a damn thing I could do to stop it now. I knew that we were flipping and I had lost all control. There was nothing I could do but send out a quick prayer that we would all make it out alive.

As the car continued to flip, my body propelled forward towards the dashboard. I could see the nose of the vehicle touch the ground underneath me. The metal of the hood of the vehicle began to crush underneath us. I felt as though I was on a salt and pepper ride in the local fair, belted in but with absolutely no control. Suddenly, my face hit the steering wheel. My body crashed forward after the buckle of my seatbelt gave out. Gravity and momentum continued to push me forward as the rear of the vehicle pointed straight up in the air. I felt my body slide underneath the dash of the car. As the front hood hit the concrete, my head smashed the dashboard and I was knocked out.

Get Out of the Car

While lying there unconscious, I was in the dark tunnel with the white light, yet again, with my mother's voice repeating the same phrase, "Go back! Go back! It's not your time." She tried to reason with me this time giving me more words, "You can't stay here. Don't come any closer. Go back. You have too much to do in your life. You can't come here. Your life will affect thousands of others, you have a job to do; you are only just getting started. Go back now before it's too late…"

Her words were so loud that I felt as though she was right beside me in the car. I suddenly realized I was back in my body lying on the ceiling of the car, on top of my passenger. I didn't know if he was alive, and was apprehensive to check. Robert was standing outside; I spotted his shoes when I looked out the right side window.

Robert exclaimed in a panic, "If you guys are still alive, you need to crawl out of the car as fast as you can. We don't know the condition of the engine and gas tank. You don't want to be stuck in the car if it catches on fire."

His voice woke me up. I didn't recognize at first where I was. I spent a few minutes getting my bearings and checked that I wasn't missing any of my body parts, as I was in severe pain and didn't know if I was trapped. I started to crawl backwards towards the driver's side window. I lightly shook Jeff's shoulder to check if he was alive, or to simply wake him up as my upper body was currently lying across him.

Jeff cried, "Get off of me! I am getting squished here!"

Jeff had a very small male frame. His whole body was tight in the small foot area in front of his former seat. Jeff was both in shock, and angry that we had been in a car accident. He was frustrated that I had landed on top of him, as it left no space for him to move out.

I wiggled my way off Jeff, and continued to crawl backwards out my driver's side window when I realized the loose glass that was barely hanging around my window. I stopped momentarily to break the glass off in order to prevent any further injury while crawling outside. The doors were crushed making them impossible to open. Jeff followed closely behind me. Fearing how the car had landed, we cautiously exited the vehicle.

Outside, we were grateful that we had all survived the car accident. We turned and looked at the car and noticed how totalled it was. We checked out how injured everyone was. Robert had sustained an eight-inch cut across his head from some broken glass. He was having problems with his balance. Jeff and I, on the other hand, seemed to have made it out completely okay, despite my having seen the tunnel and heard my mother with the incredible message of why I had to stay.

I walked around to the back of the car. I managed to reach Robert just in time to pull him off the edge of the road. He hadn't noticed how close he was standing to the highway as another car sped past us, almost hitting him.

Robert commented, "Thanks, just what I didn't need at this time! I get out of one major car accident just to be killed by another! Thanks Holly. I wish we were back in Canada right now! I can't wait to get us back home!"

I replied, "Right now, I'm just glad that we are all alive!"

Robert said, "That makes two of us."

Jeff added in, "No, that makes three of us."

He walked around to see where we had just been standing. I noticed on the far side of the four-lane highway that the same eighteen-wheeler I had noticed earlier was still sitting there. The driver was the only other person on the highway that had been near us when our accident occurred.

The adrenaline running through my veins provided me with the strength to "keep morning forward." With my previous military police experience, I knew it was important to gather all the evidence I could in case I needed to defend myself in a court of law. So, I walked over to him.

I asked, "Can you please call an ambulance?"

He replied, "I already have. Wow. Did you guys all make it out of your car? Is there anyone still in your wrecked vehicle? Are you guys all okay?"

"Yes, we are okay. We are all out of the vehicle. Nobody is left inside of the car, thank God!"

"Wow, that's amazing you guys all survived that accident! I have seen it before where people get a little bumper accident and they die. I watched you guys. Your car's rear-end flipped over its hood, and then rolled two-and-a-half times on its side; that is how you landed on the hood of your car. It was a miracle that you guys are still alive. Sorry to say this but you guys should have died. I'm totally amazed that you all made it out alive. The Lord must have been watching over you guys."

"Yep, I guess it wasn't our time!"

"You must have an angel watching over you guys! Why else would you still be alive? Hey, who was driving anyways?"

"Me!"

"God has a higher purpose for you guys! Did you fall asleep at the wheel?"

"No, I was trying to avoid the black ice. When I hit the large patch of black ice, I slammed on my brakes. I think my front wheels stopped, but the back wheels kept moving forward, pushing us and rolling our car!"

"Yeah, there is a lot of black ice out here tonight."

"I can't believe the snow out here tonight. I didn't realize it snowed in the desert."

"It doesn't normally. That's why it's the desert. We don't get wet weather down here. It's a freak snow coming from the north. Hey, where are you people from anyways?"

"We are from Canada. We are used to weather like this. We are also used to the cold."

"Yeah, I guess you would be, living way up there."

"Well, I better get back to my husband and friend. Thanks for helping us out."

"You're welcome. I will wait right here until the ambulance crew gets here. They might have some questions for me. I am your witness of the whole ordeal. They will need to know exactly what I saw. It will also be easier for them to see you with my lights on. That way you guys aren't left out here in the desert alone, you guys probably need medical care. It's windy out here and, with the low visibility, they might miss seeing you in the dark. I don't want you young people to freeze to death out here because they can't see you."

"Well, thanks so much again for your hospitality."

"Hey, no problem. Good luck to all of you. I sincerely mean that!"

"Thanks."

Before I stepped back down from his truck, I waited for a couple of cars to swiftly drive past, and walked back to our upside down vehicle. The tires were just coming to a rest. I was stunned that we had survived such a severe car accident. I had first-hand knowledge of such things with my dad being a volunteer fireman. He had explained how strange it was that the simplest of fender benders could end in death whereas people survived and crawled out of major car accidents like this one. It wasn't for me to explain or understand. I was just grateful that we had survived. The guys managed to pull out a couple of blankets and had tried to reach for their coats while I was talking with the driver of the transport truck, but to no avail. The car was too unstable on the ground. They were concerned that the smell of leaking gas meant that the car might catch fire, so they had given up. We huddled together and tried to keep warm with the blankets.

We stood about fifteen feet away from the car. I cuddled into my husband's chest to keep us both warm. While I was glad that the truck driver was willing to defend my position in regards to my driving capability; I was slightly frustrated when I realized how long we had to wait outside, freezing.

I wondered how we were going to make it home. We had no money to fly. We didn't have family members who had emergency funds that I knew of. Robert could sense I was worried.

Robert told me, "Don't worry about the girls. I'm sure they are doing fine. They are probably at your sister's, sleeping in their warm beds. We need to focus on ourselves right now. We may have some pending health concerns that we don't know we have. We have to get checked out by doctors. We can worry about getting home after seeing the doctor. Besides, I'm pretty sure my family has the funds. They can afford to help us get home."

Help Arrives

As we continued to hold each other, we heard the ambulance coming down the road. When they got there, the crew did their initial check-ups just inside the back of the ambulance. The paramedics started asking us questions about the car accident, which we couldn't answer. I pointed to the truck driver, telling the paramedic that he had seen the whole accident. "He told me that, and would like to talk to you. He is willing to answer any questions you may have about our car accident."

The leading paramedic asked her partner, "Can you take over? Are you going to be okay for a moment, if I go over to the truck driver for a few minutes? I need to ask him a few questions."

He replied, "Yes, sure."

The paramedic checked all of our vitals. He buckled me onto the gurney after assisting me into the ambulance. Robert and Jeff sat on the bench on the opposite side of the ambulance facing the gurney for the ride to the hospital.

The female paramedic returned a few minutes later, with all the information she needed. She closed the doors behind her, and we left the scene of the accident.

She focused all of her attention on me, as we were driving down the road. My body started to go into convulsions from the pain, and I was not able to answer any more of her questions. She turned to my husband.

She asked, "Is your wife pregnant?"

Robert answered, "Yes."

She went back to asking me questions. "Do you know whether you're having a girl or a boy?" I didn't respond. She raised her voice and continued, "You have to keep talking. Answer my questions, if you can."

"No, I am only three months pregnant."

"Are you going to find out what it is?"

"No, we are keeping that for a surprise. We want a boy. We already have two girls. A healthy girl would be just as great, too."

She began hooking me up to the machines to monitor both me and my baby. She noticed on the machines that my unborn child was going into fetal distress. She told her assistant who was driving to escalate our present status and reported to the hospital about our present health concerns. The male paramedic turned the emergency sirens on. The female paramedic told the driver that the baby was in fetal distress. She turned to my husband.

She said, "Sir..."

He responded, "My name's Robert."

"Well, Robert, your baby is in distress. It looks like we might lose your child." As the initial shock of the accident had passed, and the adrenaline left my body, my heart rate decreased. The paramedic checked my vitals and noticed that I was flat lining. She continued talking, "Brace yourself, Robert. It looks like we might lose both of them."

I heard what the paramedic was saying. I tried to say goodbye to my husband. I had my eyes open, but I couldn't speak. I grabbed Robert's hand and squeezed it gently. He held it for about a minute, and then the paramedic took my hand back to my body.

Having my hand being taken away from Robert zapped me out of my body. Having been in this particular scenario before, it was easy for me to crossover so quickly.

While I began to float above the ambulance, I watched the paramedic's actions. I couldn't say a word, being detached from my body, but I watched as she frantically worked on me. She ripped open the buttons on my shirt and grabbed the small paddles on the side wall of the ambulance, quickly put liquid on my chest and zapped me with the paddles. Within a split second I could see the entire surroundings. I saw my husband, Jeff, the female paramedic, my body, the inside and then the outside the ambulance, the road and the surrounding countryside.

However, when she used the defibrillator on me again, I instantly returned into my physical body with a thud, and began breathing again. As my chest lifted slightly above the gurney from my first breath, my spiritual body and physical body reunited. When I came back, I noticed that my mouth was wet. I slowly took my right hand up towards my mouth to wipe it. I instantly noticed that my whole body felt heavy and exhausted. Every inch of me hurt, and I felt a tingling sensation all over my body.

When we arrived at the hospital, the doctors did emergency tests on us to check for any possible brain damage, bleeding, or broken bones. After being approved for nonfatal complications, we were admitted into an observation area for overnight monitoring adjacent to the emergency desk.

When we woke up the next morning, after the nurses had done their morning check-ins, a volunteer offered us breakfast. I asked the volunteer, "Can I call my twin sister back in Canada? Our two daughters have been staying with her while we have been away."

The volunteer left the room temporarily to speak to our nurse, who came back with some pain killers for my husband and re-checked our vital signs. She gave me permission to have one ten-minute phone call to our family back home. I picked up the phone and dialled her number. I instantly connected with her as she picked up the phone on the first ring.

I spoke with Heidi for a few minutes informing her about our car accident, how we were doing and where we were, before I asked to speak with my daughters. However, upon my request she responded with "Don't worry about your kids, they are in safe hands. Instead, worry about where you are and how you're getting back home. Just call me as soon as you get back home to Ottawa."

Just then, the nurse returned and noticed that I was getting agitated. She told me that my time was up and I needed to get off the phone. As I hung up the phone, the nurse asked "So, how are your daughters?"

I replied, "I don't know; they aren't there. My sister is acting strange. I hope they are alright. I'm thinking that they might have gone out with other family members, who also live in London."

About an hour later, a family from the local SCA club picked us up from the hospital and drove us to a motel room for the night. Robert and I contacted his grandmother, and together we managed to arrange two connecting emergency flights back home to Ottawa the next morning. Jeff remained with the SCA members while his mother arranged for his own ticket home that night. We never saw Jeff again.

Going Home

We arrived at our doorstep at 11:00 p.m. on Saturday night, nine days after we had left Heidi's. As soon as I opened the door to our apartment in Ottawa, I dropped my bags and picked up my phone to call Heidi.

Once I got her on the phone, I exclaimed, "I am back home in Ottawa, and would like to know where my daughters are."

She responded "I called the Children's Aid Society (CAS) about their respite program on the 7th day after you left; the program that you told me about in Ottawa. I just wanted to inquire what they could do to help me with your daughters. I also told them that you and Robert went on a ten-day trip to the United States. The CAS immediately came over to my home, picked up both the girls, and labelled them as abandoned. Your girls are currently in a foster care awaiting a permanent placement Monday, unless you show up here in London at the CAS office by 9:00 a.m. Monday morning to fight for them."

I couldn't believe what I was hearing, I was devastated and asked her, "Why?"

My sister responded, "I called our oldest sister who informed me that the best solution for your girls was the London CAS respite program."

I went to bed that night not knowing if I would ever see my kids again. Within a few hours of tossing and turning all night and waking up early, I had packed another bag, and began the long seven block walk between our apartment at 327 Cambridge Street, Ottawa towards the Greyhound station on Catherine Street to get on any bus heading towards Toronto and eventually to my kids in London.

My heart sank to the pit of my stomach as I mustered up all the inner strength I needed to begin my journey to fight for the right to have custody of my own children. Knowing Robert had just lost his job and we were moving into his mother's attic apartment in Peterborough, our chances to regain custody didn't look good. My feelings were running frantic. I was afraid that I might lose my children and any chance of meeting any future grandchildren all because I went on a long overdue honeymoon with my husband Robert.

When I arrived in London late Sunday afternoon on the 10th day since our original departure, my brother picked me up at the station and took me to his house for the duration of the CAS and the ensuing court case. I arrived in the Court Office by exactly 9:00 a.m. to dispute my case. Within a few minutes, they found out about my status with the CAS in Ottawa.

The CAS in London requested a short recess to review the file and speak to somebody in the CAS Ottawa office about my file. We reconvened about ten minutes later with a fresh perspective from Ottawa. Ottawa had stated that they were working with me on the respite program trying to get me some sleep. The Court observed that I had been doing all I could to provide for my children to my own detriment. Therefore, they decided that I should not be punished for trying so hard, and that I should have my children returned to me immediately and have my file closed after just a short period of volunteer supervision, and review and approval from the CAS.

The court case was concluded with the decision that I would be allowed to see my children right away and take them home in three days, after the paperwork was completed in their office.

When I arrived back home to Ottawa with the kids, I finished packing and left in two days for Robert's mother's apartment in Peterborough.

6

SHOCKING EXPERIENCE

It matters not how straight the gate,
How charged with punishments the scroll,
I am the master of my fate;
I am captain of my soul!

—William E. Henley

Our New Home

While living with Robert's mother, we found it overcrowded and the CAS agreed. We applied for housing. Our application was accepted as soon as our third child was born, and we moved into a geared-to income townhouse.

In early October 1990, we were experiencing the occasional warm day, which turned to cool evenings and nights. The windows were open to let in the fresh air and optimize the indoor air quality for my three daughters at 2 months, 22 months, and 3 years old. At this point my girls were very full of energy and could be quite a handful.

It was soon after moving to our own place that I separated from my husband Robert. The girls and I lived alone, in a low-rent housing townhouse in the southeast area of Peterborough, Ontario.

Early in the morning was the ideal time to gather all of the laundry before the children woke up and required all of my attention and supervision to attend to their needs. Once they were up, my day would be all about keeping them happy, healthy and entertained. The windows were left open in the basement where the washer and dryer were propped up on wooden plank boards. The clean air was invigorating to a tired mother sorting seemingly endless laundry into colors for different loads. This morning several large piles of clothes were spread all over the cement floor in the basement, ready for washing, when I headed back upstairs to mind my three daughters.

Six months after separating from Robert, I met a fisherman named Murphy, and we started dating long distance. He was coming into town the next night to pick us up for the weekend to take us to Brighton, Ontario. He had no washing machine of his own, so our laundry needed to be cleaned and ready to go before he picked us up.

My entire day was spent trying to balance completing the laundry and taking care of my children. The girls played in our living room with their toys, or went down and played in the neighbourhood community park. A local friend and I tag-teamed with childcare as we shared chores and watched each other's children throughout the day.

Even though it had been a busy day chasing after my children, I knew it was important to finish the laundry before I could go to bed. At about 9:00 p.m., I lay down on my couch for a moment of rest and relaxation before heading back downstairs to do more laundry. I settled down to watch an entertainment show geared more towards adults rather than my daughters' age group. Feeling completely worn out, I barely had strength to get up for Elizabeth's last feeding before I retired for the night. Before I knew it I started to get comfortable on the couch and found myself drifting off into a deep sleep.

Shocking Experience

About two hours later, Elizabeth (Lizzie) woke up screaming for her bottle. I was stunned awake instantly, and bolted upstairs before she woke her two older siblings and a crying match broke out between the girls.

When I flew off the couch, I noticed a large pool of water at the base of the stairs. I realized a rainstorm had started. There was considerable wind and rain, and the fall leaves blew everywhere. The large living room window was about six inches open, allowing for a puddle of water to accumulate in our living room. To my dismay, I found I was unable to get it closed, so for the time being I grabbed a small towel that was sitting on my living room table and threw it on the water.

Lizzie started to cry even louder. I quickly got to the fridge and grabbed a bottle, and warmed it in the microwave. I closed the kitchen window in time to hear the microwave buzzer go off. Running past the window in the front living room, I attempted to close it again, but it remained stuck open. I quickly remarked, with the bottle in hand, "Arg! I'll have to shut this window when I come back!" and yelled, "I am coming Elizabeth!"

Upstairs, I picked up Lizzie and started feeding her the bottle. Luckily she was fed in time to keep her from waking her two older sisters. I looked at the amount of water on the girls' window sill. The water was going down their wall. By the looks of things, the puddle had been accumulating on the girls' floor for a few hours. I continued to hold Lizzie, as I went to fetch a full body towel to wipe up the floor. Using my feet, I moved the towel around to mop up the mess. I quickly moved around the top floor, closing the remaining two windows. The temperature must have dropped when the rain started to pour. I was surprised that Lizzie's older sisters didn't wake up due to the cold and damp air in their room. I placed additional blankets on each of the girls, and turned up the heat in our townhouse.

Now fed and happy, Lizzie fell back asleep when I put her back in her crib with a blanket. Upon leaving the room, I went to the bathroom and gathered more body towels. I started to clean up the water puddles that remained in front of the previously open windows. My cotton mattress that lay on the floor in front of a window panel had gotten soaked.

After about a half an hour of trying to absorb the water on my bed I was finally able to make progress. I took off the blankets and remade the bed and put blankets on only half of the bed to allow for part of it to start drying. The girls' rooms felt as though they were becoming warmer, and a check of the temperature showed that the rooms were coming back up to normal. I gathered the wet blankets, sheets, and towels from the floor.

It was most efficient to toss the sheets and towels lightly down the stairs, and kick down the blankets. This motion was repeated two or three more times to get all the laundry down the thirteen steps to the main floor. When I reached the living room, I used one of the towels from the pile and cleaned up the puddle. I continued this process from window to window on the ground floor. Upon reaching the doorway to the basement, all the wet linens were on the basement staircase, so I turned on the lights to avoid tripping. I tried to get the linens to the basement back corner.

The washer and dryer were located at the back corner directly under the open window. I was expecting to see the linens landing on the cool concrete floor, but instead I noticed that the toys and linens were floating in about six inches of water. I could hear that my washing machine was moving on its wood planks. I could also feel the cool air coming from the window. The cold weather was making me shiver and not think straight.

The Flood
There was a thin rope attached to a pull chain light switch and I had to stumble around in the dark to try to find it hanging down in the middle of the basement ceiling. I could still hear the washing machine in its spin cycle and was afraid that the machine was going to fall off the wood and land on its side. I wasn't sure how to quickly and safely solve this problem.

The washing machine had moved over a foot in distance from its original spot. I thought to myself that if I didn't get to it soon there was going to be an even bigger problem. I began to move the clothes and toys a good foot from the middle of the concrete floor's draining system, which had been blocked for a while.

Within a few minutes the washing machine had shaken a few more inches towards me. It was now standing on the cold grey concrete floor and surrounded by six inches of water. The water on the floor was rising by two different sources; one was from the open window, and the other was from the blocked drainage pipe from the washing machine. The water had started to drain after I removed the pile of clothes and toys, however, the floor was still covered with water and the machine was inching closer and closer towards its edge. I became afraid that I wouldn't be able to lift the machine, so, I impulsively pulled the washing machine's plug. Immediately, as I grabbed the plug with my left hand, I felt an electric shock of pain traveling up my arm!

All ability to move my muscles was instantly gone. My hand seemed to seize around the plug. I tried but could not let it go. The rapid pain of electric shock came piercing through my entire body. It traveled up my arm and into my heart. I could feel my chest fluttering. Every part of my body was shaken with the force of electric currents. I started to shake violently. I could see the lights turning on and off during this process.

As the force of electricity travelled through my entire body, I started to feel an extreme amount of pain that I had never felt before. My brain felt like it was frying and my heart swirled. I could see for only a millisecond a vague resemblance of myself standing in water. My body started to convulse as this electrical source went through me. The wire became attached to me. I no longer had the power to think. Electrical shocks of over 23 amps were travelling through my body.

Suddenly, I heard a man's voice yell at me. I sensed that my guardian angel was a dim shadow of a man standing beside me. Even though I couldn't see him completely, I could hear him very clearly call out, "Let go of the plug now or you will die!" I cried out to him, "Please, help me! I can't let go of the plug! My hand seems to be glued to it. I want to live! If I die tonight, who will take care of my kids?"

I was then outside of my physical body, seeing myself as a second party standing there. I could feel the electric shocks going through my body at first. Soon, as they hit my heart and became too painful, I seemed to disjoin my spiritual body from my physical body. My guardian angel was there even though I knew physically I lived alone with my children. I felt desperate to stay alive for my children, who were sleeping two floors above me.

My physical body separated from my spiritual body and I watched the scene from a distance beside my guardian angel. We patiently waited to see if we could leave this physical body standing there. It was as though an empty mirror of myself stood there being electrocuted. Temporarily disconnected from my physical body, I felt as though I wanted to leave this realm and go with my spiritual teacher somewhere else. My spiritual self anxiously awaited, like a little girl, for permission to leave my physical body to die.

Curiosity toward my physical shell was all I experienced now. My spiritual body didn't have any emotional ties to the flesh—no impulse to diminish the situation; no sense of urgency; void of any emotion towards my own physical shell of flesh that was standing right in front of me. I could watch the whole ordeal; I didn't feel the shaking or foam that was coming out of the mouth of my physical counterpart.

Time seemed to stand still. It was waiting for me to make a decision. Everything seemed to ask whether I wanted to stay or go. Hours seemed to pass within a few minutes, when I finally came back. It seemed like I had just woken up. I was a little taken aback at what had just transpired. Was the situation real?

My electric shock experience was real! I had just been electrocuted. I could tell because of the evidence that lay close to me. I saw the plug. I must have dropped it when my soul re-entered my body and I flew abruptly twelve feet across the room and hit the back of my head against the concrete floor. This must have realigned my spiritual body with my physical body and woke me up, returning me to a conscious awareness.

When I woke up I was on a cold and damp floor. It was no longer covered in water. I realized that I must have been there for a while. I was freezing. I regained my bearings, picked myself up, and closed the window. I used all of my strength and two hands on the railing to drag myself back up the stairs. I grabbed the door handle while teetering at the top of the staircase, closing the door behind me in order to prevent my daughters from entering the basement.

The severe effects of electric volts pulsing through my body continued to be felt inside of me through all of this. My body began to ache with serious pain. I was feeling bruised and sore; every part of my body felt as though it had been through a major athletic race. It was unbearable. I had pitch black markings on my hand where I had held the plug.

My body felt about two hundred pounds heavier. I was aware of my surroundings. Life seemed a lot simpler as I found out—yet again—how easy it is to have one's life taken away. Breathing in a sigh of relief that I had made it out of another traumatic situation, I walked back upstairs. I wanted to know how much time had passed since I had been lying on the floor in the basement. I checked the clock on the microwave, but it was blinking. The alarm clock beside the TV was blinking.

The Children

Questions about my children came racing into my head. Were my children all right? Had they woken up? I continued up the stairs and checked on my girls, making sure they were safe. My daughters were safe and asleep in their beds.

Having reached the bedroom landing after checking on my girls, I stumbled towards my bedroom. I just wanted to lie down on my bed and be close to my children; I didn't know what the next few minutes or hours held for me. As I continued to feel every nerve of my body sparking, I could feel tiny volts penetrating in my head. I had the worst headache that I had ever felt in my entire life. My breathing had changed; I was aware of everything in my home and surroundings.

The next day, I watched my children play with the neighbourhood children. I talked to the parents in the community. They all mentioned that six houses in the attached row lost their electricity at the time that I was electrocuted. For the next several days, I continued to feel the presence of my guardian angel remaining around me, despite how ridiculously unintelligent I had been to cause my own potential demise.

Back to School

At the end of the six months, the girls and I rented a house on Ontario Street in Brighton. We lived with Murphy for the first year, but by the end of the year, the girls and I took a smaller rental house and Murphy took up residence with his old roommate near the shores of Gosport, a subdivision of Brighton.

I applied to the nearby college and was accepted to attend Loyalist College's two-year Information Systems Technology Program for the January 1993 class, in Belleville, Ontario.

At the end of the year, I was walking down the hallway of my college when a fire alarm went off. I walked outside and bumped into my tutor, who was helping me learn basic English grammar in order to create the reports I needed for my teachers. While standing outside, he introduced me to another fellow named Keith.

Keith appeared to me as a handsome, intelligent person with a cheerful personality, who caught my interest right away. We spoke briefly, but during our conversation we learned that we attended different sections of the same program. When the fire drill was over, we had forgotten to exchange phone numbers and lost contact with each other.

A full year later, I had a repeating dream that I was about to walk into a classroom that had two doors and I would end up sitting right beside a man who would change my life forever. Incidentally, that dream became a reality when I ended up sitting beside the man whom I met during the fire drill the year before, Keith. These dreams predicted my future relationship with him as well as where we would eventually live.

I broke up with Murphy and I moved to Belleville, to be closer to my college. This reduced travel costs and increased my time with my daughters, who were now 2, 4 and 5 years old. During major assignments and exam preparation, I arranged for a babysitter so I could study at school. Some students didn't appreciate the fact that sometimes I had to drag my little girls to class, when I was unable to find a babysitter for my older children on P.A. days.

As I predicted, I had started dating Keith and had introduced him to all three of my daughters. We graduated together from Loyalist College and a year later, we moved in with each other in Ottawa, where I had predicted two years earlier we would live.

Keith and I got married on July 2nd, 1999, on my stepsister's birthday. The day was beautiful for an outside wedding in the rose garden of the Experimental Farm. The pastor had to temporarily stop our service as the Snowbirds flew over our heads and the noise became so loud nobody could hear.

7

PLUMMETING ELEVATOR

Falling from cloud nine, crashing from the high, I'm letting go tonight.

—Katy Perry, *Wide Awake*

My Dream Job

I began working at various odd jobs around Ottawa while I applied for a federal government job. It was my dream to work for the RCMP, and within six months of passing the government tests, I received the first of three government positions. I applied for the RCMP, but had some trouble getting in because, as unheard of as it sounds, my twin sister and I have identical fingerprints, which slowed down the process of my employment. So, I started working for Human Resources Development Canada for three months.

Once my fingerprints were cleared, I received the first of many six month contracts as a civilian clerk within The Royal Canadian Mounted Police: one in the Criminal Police Information Check Department and the other in the Firearms Verifications Civic Officer Department.

After working there for two-and-a-half years, I received a pink slip, informing me of my dismissal, as there was a political downsize in that department and many contracts were not extended. After several weeks of searching various sectors, I received an offer from the Public Works and Government Services (PWGSC) Department that specialized in the maintenance and repair of elevators in Ottawa's Government Buildings.

When I started my new job at PWGSC, my schedule changed from an evening shift to full-time days. This finally gave me time to spend with my family in the evenings. That was facilitated even more when I managed to rent a parking spot in the basement of my new office by late January. This allowed me to arrive home sooner to my daughters, than what he bus would have allowed.

Plummeting Elevator
The morning of February 15th, 2002, started off as usual. I drove my husband to work before heading to the office. I parked in the basement, boarded the middle elevator, and pushed the button for the sixth floor. I settled into a spot in the back left corner of the elevator, expecting to have other people board on the main floor. I didn't realize that it was 8:05 a.m. and most of the employees in the building had already arrived to work.

Then, the moment of terror that changed my life forever began. As soon as the doors closed, the elevator started accelerating upwards too fast. I braced myself. Clutched in my right hand was the cane I used to support my left knee, which was injured in a previous military incident. I tried to grab the bar on the wall with my left hand, but it miraculously slipped and my left arm became wedged between the bar and the elevator wall. It was always a fear of mine to fall from a great height. As I looked up, I realized that my fear was actually occurring; the elevator was malfunctioning with me inside of it. The floor numbers were flashing by: 2, 5, and 8. Having graduated in Information and Technology, I understood some of the complexities and malfunctions that occurred within the computers of such systems. The irony was not lost on me.

I reached the top two floors with no indication that the elevator was going to stop. I wondered if I was going to fly out of the roof of the building like the elevator in *Charlie and the Chocolate Factory*. I had nothing left to do but pray for my family and myself. Then, the elevator suddenly gave a quick jolt for a split second, and it began to plummet with just as much speed. Now more than ever, I tried to reach for the emergency button, but my left arm was still wedged. I had no idea how I was going to get through the descent.

The increasing velocity of the elevator pushed my body up towards the ceiling. My body was starting to levitate, as the elevator fell faster than gravity could keep me grounded. I started screaming for help, not knowing if anybody could hear me. Scenes of my life, the precious significant times and the most meaningful moments of my existence, flashed before my eyes. It was like watching a quick film of the people, places, and things that had occurred up to that moment. These pictures resembled an old 50 mm quick film, except they were in colour. All the emotions associated with these visual representations also came flooding back. It was as though someone has spent significant effort arranging this film, like a movie in the cinema. However, I was the only audience for this performance.

A heavenly, peaceful voice whispered to me. My guardian angel, Oliver, appeared in front of me and stated, "You're going to be okay." I realized then that my pinned arm was, in fact, saving my life. I knew my guardian angel had protected me.

For a few seconds, I had a sensation of contentment, and I was at ease in my moment of sheer terror. I glanced at the numbers again. The numbers descended just as fast: 8, 4, 2. Suddenly, there was a loud explosive sound as the elevator brakes grabbed at the second floor with a tremendous force that shook the whole elevator. I plunged with both feet onto the floor with an intensity that sent vibrations through my entire body. My knees buckled, my teeth ground together, and my shoulder slammed the wall on my right. I felt instant pain in every nerve of my body. I was a rag doll at the mercy of this runaway elevator. My left elbow was still stuck behind the bar and the rest of my body was smashed against the wall.

I was feeling the intense sensation of what had just transpired. I was even more desperate to reach for the emergency call button. However, no sooner had I believed that this ordeal was over, did I feel movement again. In my immediate fright, there were doubts in my mind about the spirit's message that I was going to be all right. Now, the elevator was climbing again. I wondered if this was the start of another plunge. I feared the worst.

This time though, the elevator climbed at the expected pace. It stopped on the floor that I had originally requested. The doors opened as though what had just occurred had realigned it. I felt severe pain in every part of my body, including my teeth. I managed to get my arm out from between the bar and the wall, allowing me to move as quickly as I could to disembark from the metal box of terror. Mentally and physically shaken from what had just transpired, I felt completely unstable on my feet. The fear of the elevator letting go again gave me the incentive to leave from the metal box, despite the presence of injuries that should have held me immobile.

In a State of Shock

I was empowered to walk off the chamber of danger. As with the car accident, the adrenaline was coursing through my body and I was able to "keep moving forward." I turned to my right. I was about five feet away from a safety and security clerk. She told me to go see my boss. A few minutes later the same lady came running over to my boss's desk and said, "Did, you say you fell six floors in the elevator?" I responded, "Yes, that's correct". My boss was trying to get me to sit on her chair, but it was too painful. The two of them brought me to an empty office and laid me on the floor until the ambulance arrived. As I lay on the floor, I succumbed to the pain and I started crying and screaming from the cramping my body was enduring. By the time the ambulance arrived, I was going in and out of shock, and I was in excruciating torment. I vaguely remember my boss giving what details she could to the paramedics. I was informed that I would be taken to the Ottawa Civic Hospital, before they wheeled me out on the gurney. I was fearful of taking another elevator ride, as now, for the first time in my life, I was terrified of handing my life over to a machine, especially one that minutes earlier had traumatized me and almost killed me. I made sure that I wasn't in the middle elevator again. The paramedic placed his clipboard against the gripping handle and the bed of the gurney in order to provide me a place to rest my feet when they rolled me into a different elevator.

The Turning Point

When we got outside the office, I noticed a store's awning that hadn't seemed to affect me until that moment. The awning read, "The Turning Point." I wondered if this was a sign that my life as I knew it was completed, and I wondered what the spirit world wanted me to note from this strange message. Although the store had been there for decades, why was it not until then that I had noticed it?

The emergency crew loaded me in the back of the ambulance, as my boss was allowed to sit beside me and comfort me on the ride to the hospital. When we arrived at the hospital about ten minutes later, they started wheeling me into the emergency department and my boss said, "I will call your husband."

My husband later reported that it scared him when she said on the phone, "Your wife is still alive, but she needs you. Come quickly to the hospital."

I was given a first response medical examination and several series of X-rays. I was diagnosed with 80% muscle damage. I had no apparent broken bones, but I had two protruding discs between the T9-T10 and the L5-S1 vertebrae. I was told that with 80% of my muscles affected, I should prepare for a long haul as it takes muscles twice as long to heal as broken bones. I lost an inch in height, as doctors discovered that my neck bent into a "C" shape during the accident. I was lucky it didn't snap completely. I had tendonitis in both my shoulders and severe muscle spasms and cramping throughout my whole body, including my mouth. The doctors that released me stated that I was very fortunate to survive such an ordeal, that many people had gone through less and hadn't made it, and that I must have been here for a reason. By noon the same day, and in the care of my family, I was given a prescription for my pain. I had three days off work with a requisition to see my family doctor Monday morning, for more extensive care while I leaned against various structures, walls or my daughters for walking assistance.

Our Meeting

After my general practitioner's appointment, I met with my former supervisor and the TSAA worker who had inspected the elevator directly after the accident.

He stated, "Right after the accident, I went up to the elevator's gauges that morning to inspect it, which are located at the top of the building. Its speedometer read that it had reached a maximum of 125 kph. He said that he was surprised that I had lived, as it would have been equivalent to a race car driver, driving straight into a cement wall on the race track, feet first. It was later found out that the people on the second and third floors reported that the building shook, making the people inside feel as though they were experiencing either tremors or an earthquake on both of the floors closest to the impact.

Prescription and Rehab

By the end of two weeks, my doctor had prescribed me Tylenol 3 for pain, which barely worked. So I felt everything—the pain, the muscle cramps, and the overall inflammation. He prescribed me a back brace, walker, sock strap, reach bar, walking canes, and a hospital bed. Eventually, my doctor put me on Fentanyl. He wrote letters for my employer for permanent disability and to the License Bureau for a handicap permit. He also arranged aqua fitness, continuous massage therapy, and a psychologist. I went to neurologist appointments for my muscle spasms. All treatments were to continue as my body healed.

By the end of the month, I went back to the Emergency Department at the Civic Hospital, as I couldn't move my right leg—it had become paralyzed. I was lying on a gurney in the hospital emergency department triage for a week, wondering why I wasn't given a bed or a room upstairs. The nurses told me that I was waiting for a bed at the Ottawa Rehab Unit in the General Hospital and, therefore, would not be admitted to their hospital. I was lying only ten feet from the emergency desk, receiving regular shots of morphine intravenously; the pain in my back was so severe that I couldn't bear the intensity. The cramps seemed to have shortened my muscles, bending me backwards, putting me into a reverse "C" shaped curve as it continued to bend my torso. I was afraid that my spine might not handle the contracting and bending motion. My muscles were reacting to the strain it had been put under. The medical staff told me that my body was trying to self-adjust from the accident.

As I lay on the gurney, the nursing staff put a wheeled bed-pan chair at the end of my bed so that I could go to the bathroom. It was embarrassing as I heard the other patients in the room make comments, like "I hope she hurries up." As I was dragging my right leg back onto the bed, a nurse came rushing over to me and accused me of faking, stating that she saw me moving my leg. I was appalled. Who in their right mind would want to lie on a gurney for days in the emergency room, when they had a loving family, a government job, and a semi-detached beautiful home in the suburbs—a home that as a child I could only dream of having one day? I was visibly upset in response to her comment, and stated "I am sorry, but my leg is attached to my body and it seems to be dragging along with the rest of my body," as I pulled myself back up to the head of the gurney; "now could I please have my pain killers; I am in a lot of pain."

By the end of the week, the Rehab Specialist came over to visit me from the General Hospital. He spoke to the nurses and doctors about my case, spoke to my husband and daughter Lizzie, and then told me that he had to test me for being paralyzed before he moved me to his hospital. He began by examining my left leg, poking me with some kind of pin or needle. I felt every inch that he lightly poked into my left leg, but then he was doing something else and I couldn't feel any pain. He came back up towards my face on the gurney, and I asked him if he was going to test my right leg. He responded, stating that he had just completed my leg test and that I was indeed paralyzed. He would have to move me to the Ottawa Rehab Centre, where a newly opened bed was waiting for me. I needed to become accustomed to being away from my home while we spent the length of time necessary for me to get used to my new lifestyle. He was very pleasant and easy to speak with, and told my husband, who was standing on the other side of me, that this could take some adjustment, and that I would have everything I needed at the Rehab Centre to deal with the emotional, physical and mental encouragement I would require during the process.

I was devastated; my emotions and thoughts ran wild. I was paralyzed, my right leg was gone, and my life as an independent and strong woman was gone too. How could this have happened to me when all I did was go to work and board an elevator, as millions of people do every day?

Now my life, as I knew it, was gone.

I was boarded into the ambulance and taken to the Rehab Centre during a very long and bumpy ride, which took about twenty minutes. Over the last several large bumps, I prayed for God to release me from the burdens that now surrounded me and from the pain I felt. To my surprise, due to the vibration from the bumps, I felt the tension in my back release, I was no longer cramped in one position, and I felt the sensation in my leg return. By the time the paramedics parked in front of the Rehab Centre,

I had unbuckled my seatbelt on the gurney, and I was standing inside the ambulance. The ambulance crew were amazed, looked at each other with shock and said, "This is a miracle. You were paralyzed and now you are walking." I asked them if they wouldn't mind helping me down from the back of the ambulance, and I asked where I was supposed to meet my husband and daughter.

I still had to report to what was supposed to be my bed and wait for my family, the nurse to admit me, and the doctor to re-examine me before I could go home. Everybody commented that it was a miracle and that I was very blessed to be healed, as it can take years for a condition like mine to heal, if it ever does. The nurse admitted me, the doctor examined me and then my chart was closed, and I was released within the hour.

The Recovery Process

Over the next eight years, my body went through a considerable ordeal to recover. The first few weeks, I lodged on the first floor of our house. While I waited for my hospital bed to arrive, our dining room was turned into a makeshift bedroom with a lazy boy chair that was broken (my husband and daughter found it on somebody's lawn during one of the city's leave and pickup days), a TV, and a stand with a few books. I relearned how to walk after becoming partially paralyzed within the first month. I was put on suicide watch for the first six months.

Time lingered every second. I wondered why I was still alive, why I had been given such a nasty blow in life, and what my purpose was. I continued to pray and I remembered Gabriel's forgiveness and his explanation of my purpose. I needed to rely on that message to get me through, even though every inch of my body screamed in severe pain as even breathing became excruciating each time my chest rose and lowered. The pain and lack of ability to move made it completely impossible to climb the stairs, so I lived encumbered in a fully reclining, broken, lazy-boy. I wondered, if the chair gave out would I be able to pick myself back up?

During the first year, I couldn't sit and spent lengthy periods of time shuffling around or lying down. Even though I could recline on a heating pad in that broken lazy-boy, it took me over a year before I could sit down at the kitchen table with my family to eat. Sitting in a regular chair had become impossible for any length of time. Sitting was strictly reserved for driving, where the heating system in the driver's seat allowed my back to remain relaxed as it prevented the muscles from contracting. This allowed me to reach my appointments. I had become accustomed to the loss of independence. Self-dignity was scarcely manageable, while I depended on my husband and children's generosity to help me with my self-care needs. My back spasms remained intense and I went to several out-of-hospital treatment offices and then straight back home to my lazy-boy, waiting for me in our dining room. As the "turning point" in my life, I learned to open-up my feelings, express my emotions, and start trusting others and count on others to get me through. Up to this point in my life, I had been going through the phases of my life without any real connection to anyone. Now had to become instantly and totally dependent on others. I felt like a total burden on my family, which heightened my depression even more.

My Family

Eventually, when my bed arrived, I moved upstairs with my family's help as they continued to attend to me and provide all the things I needed as well as taking care of their own outlets of work and school. I remained in my bed, grinding my teeth from the sharp pain that encompassed my entire body. For much of the time, I was left alone; depressed, and hungry, unable to obtain any food, as I was incapable of walking downstairs to the kitchen. My family would be so busy rushing around to catch their bus or go to work, that they had forgotten how much I really needed their assistance to eat. Being hyperglycemic and not able to reach the food in the kitchen, I had a few seizures while waiting for them to get home.

My regular routine consisted of sliding out of my hospital bed in order to crawl like a baby to our master bathroom, a few feet away from the end of my bed; crawling onto the toilet and back off once finished, crawling back onto the floor in order to re-enter my bed. It took all of my strength to pull myself back onto the medical bed that we had to order with a prescription from my doctor.

One morning after the family had left, my mouth became so tight that I was unable to open it. My jaw was tightening and it clamped shut. Eventually, in order just to breathe, I had to use both of my hands and pry my fingers into my mouth and pull as hard as I could in opposite directions. I ended up breaking my TMJ jawbone on the right side of my mouth, where I had hit my face against the elevator.

I wanted to give up hope of ever recovering and end my life so that I would no longer be a burden on my family. I became upset, angry, and frustrated, yelling out at him, or to myself, when I remembered what my spirit guide said to me during the accident, "You will be okay!" I am sure my neighbours, if they had seen me during that moment, would have thought I was crazy. I proceeded to ask my spirit guide, "Do you really think this is okay?! Well, if you had asked my opinion, I wouldn't have said that this is okay!" But, then it dawned on me. I wasn't dead, although I should have been. I was no longer paralyzed, which I should have been. I was actually okay. I was at home with my family and my children hadn't lost their mother. I was alive, I was still here, and knowing my track record, it was just a matter of time before I would be back to the old me. I just had to be patient.

With my family surrounding me and encouraging me to fight through the pain one day at a time, I knew I would get better. Our girls had come to know me as a fighter, somebody that didn't give up easily, although this was going to be one of the biggest fights of my life. I knew that my girls and Keith had stepped up and would assist me with my showering, dressing, walking, eating, and the increased chores around our home.

It took me ten-and-a-half years to recover. I spent two years in bed. It took me six months before being prescribed a 75 g morphine patch; a year before I could sit down at the dinner table and eat supper with the rest of the family or dress myself; two-and-a-half years before I felt comfortable entering crowded places like shopping malls; three years to move from a walker to two canes; four years of counselling to take another elevator ride; and nine-and-a-half years before I was to be able to bend and touch my feet or to put on my own footwear. In order to be able to remove the morphine patch, I had to wean myself gradually—reducing my first patch from 75 g to 50 g after two and half years, living on 50 g for the next six years until the last year when I lived on 25 g for six months—before I could completely stop using any morphine patches. After so much time, I finally got healthy enough to walk, sit and stand; able enough to rejoin everyday society and feel like myself again. Despite still having my physical limitations, including daily, minor flare-ups, I was always mindful to just how far I had come.

In 2011, my middle daughter gave birth to a son, as foretold by Gabriel years earlier; this child was born on May 4th, 2011. However, things have a way of working out differently than initially planned. Due to complications in my daughter's life, by the time Gordon was two months old, Keith and I became his full-time parents.

Eventually, my husband Keith and I separated, but remained great friends and neighbours. In September 2014, I was awarded sole guardianship of my grandson—the fourth child shown to me by Archangel Gabriel.

CONCLUSION

My personal motto is "keep moving forward." This is because I know very intimately that life is full of second chances. You may not face a second chance that comes to you after almost dying, but you should know that it doesn't take something so extreme to get you on the right path in life. For most, their second chance comes when they've made a simple choice to live again, differently. When we look at it that way, every day is a new chance to do better. My life has led me to help others and raise my grandson, Gordon, for which I am truly grateful.

My life has led me on the path to write this book in order to spread the message that "we are not alone," to provide comfort to those who are suffering, to uplift where possible, and to provide a message of encouragement where needed. I am here to help others connect with their spiritual loved ones who have gone before us, to teach others that we can connect to the spiritual realm, and to help them build confidence in themselves to "keep moving forward." When I am not writing, reading, or spending time on stage speaking, I always look forward to spending quality time with my favourite little guy, Gordon.

The opportunity to embrace our true calling, or to change our life for the better, is promised to us with each new day. We all have the potential to rise up and move past any traumatic situation and find a life that is truly worth living.

It is my hope for you that my experiences give you pause to think about what it would take to make you analyze your life. It is much safer and healthier to use daily practices, such as meditation, affirmations, or journaling to reflect on your life and choose the path that is right for you.

This is exactly why I've shared my stories and become a professional speaker—to give people inspiration, spiritual messages, and to motivate people past what holds them back from accomplishing their true callings. While I want to connect others to their loved ones on the other side, I am here to also provide spiritual guidance for those who seek their own knowledge, and to show others that we are not alone and can gain a spiritual connection with the universe.

During my life, I have come to realize that our soul's journey can expand over multiple lifetimes. We can learn where we are going by coming to a better understanding of those lives we have left behind. Throughout my life, I have gained very prominent insight into death, reincarnation, and Heaven by my near-death experiences, where I returned from the other side. I hope that I have given you a different perspective of what awaits you on the other side, and I hope that you find peace as you move closer to the end of your own life's journey.

Please stay positive, know that you are not alone in the universe and remember to always "keep moving forward!"

Holly A. Kline

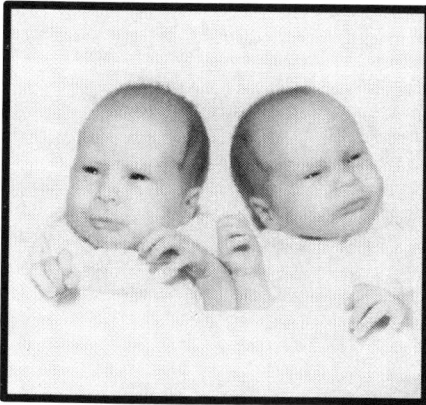

*Holly (left) and sister
Heidi (right) 1966
——Newborn*

*Holly (right) and sister
Heidi (left) 1968
——2 Years Old*

*Holly (left) and sister
Heidi (right) 1970
——4 Years Old*

127

*Holly 1976
—10 Years Old*

*Holly 1982
—15 Years Old*

*Holly 1983
——16 Years Old*

*Holly (left), Stephine (top),
Jaccinta-Marie (right),
Elizabeth (bottom) 1994
——26 Years Old*

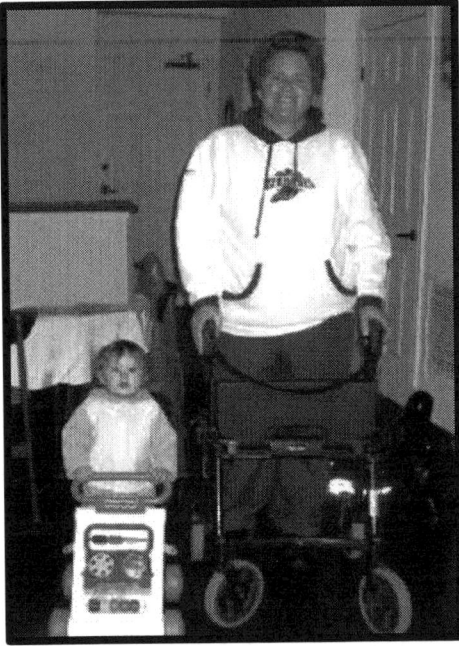

Holly (right) and granddaughter Jasmine (left) 2008 — 37 Years Old

Holly's grandson Gordon 2012

NOTES

ACKNOWLEDGEMENTS

To my family, through your enormous encouragement, initial editing, love, patience, understanding, and your continuous support of me in my life's journey, with your permission, I share our special songs: for my twin sister, Heidi Kline (Phil Collins – *Against All Odds*); Keith Thomsen (Sarah McLachlan – *I Will Remember You*); my three daughters and sons-in-law, Stephine & James Ricker (Lauren Alaina – *Like My Mother Does*), Jaccinta-Marie (Mike & The Mechanics – *The Living Years*), and Elizabeth & Tim Hann (Tim McGraw – *My Little Girl*). Dedicated to my four blessed grandchildren: Jasmine, Victoria (Vikkie), James, and especially Gordon (Sarah McLachlan – *Angel*).

I thank my close friends, Diane Paquette (Proof Reader), Linda Heritage (Counsellor), Endera Publishing, Steve Lowell (International Keynote Speaker), Anil Agrawal (Business & Marketing Coach), and others. Your encouragement to pursue my dreams, despite great adversities, gave me the inner strength I needed to pause, recollect my thoughts and push forward to see this book come to completion.

A special thanks goes out to my mother. Even though you weren't there to support to me in life, you always kept your promise to be there for me, my children and my grandchildren beyond life's vail. You have restored my faith in the spirit world, shown me that our lives have a soul-purpose, proven that it is never too late to show your true feelings and that love reaches beyond all boundaries. You had a difficult life, which you shared in part with us, but you always taught us to look for the positive in even the darkest of times. For you, one of your favorite songs: Soheil Koushan - One Tin Soldier.

ABOUT THE AUTHOR

Holly Ann Kline was born in London, Ontario on November 24, 1966. She and her twin sister were the fourth and fifth children in the Kline household. Holly lived through a traumatic childhood and is a survivor of severe child abuse. She was able to put herself through military training and become a Master Corporal in the Canadian Military and serve as a civil servant until an unfortunate elevator accident put her out of commission and forced her to rethink her life.

Throughout her life, she faced several life-threatening experiences that reinforced her connection with the spiritual world. When young, she did not share her spiritual experiences and often felt isolated and afraid. Over time, she went from experiencing the spirits arriving unexpectedly to being able to see, hear, and receive messages after calling forth the spirits at her own will. She began sharing messages she received with people she cared about, and soon learned that this ability was not shameful, but a gift.

Holly now practices as a psychic medium, author and motivational speaker who has devoted herself to inspiring people with the retelling of her own life story. Through her traumatic life events and many anecdotes about her experiences with the spiritual world, she has honed her psychic abilities in order to bring hope to others. Holly lives by the slogan of 'keep moving forward.'

Holly now resides in Ottawa, Ontario with Gordon, her grandson whom she has legal guardianship of. She is the author of *7 Times Saved: How One Woman's Spiritual Connections to the Other Side Saved Her Life.* and more books that will be published in the near future.

Feb 13/
2016

To:
gobinder

Thank you for
your support
I hope you
find this
another Cheryl,

Sincerely,

Made in the USA
Charleston, SC
16 January 2016